Walker Percy:
A Comprehensive
Descriptive Bibliography

WALKER PERCY, MANDEVILLE SEA WALL, 1987

ALL PHOTOS THROUGHOUT WERE TAKEN BY RHODA K. FAUST

Walker Percy: A Comprehensive Descriptive Bibliography

Linda Whitney Hobson

Introduction by Walker Percy

Faust Publishing Company
New Orleans
1988

Library of Congress Catalog Card Number: 87-080959
Hobson, Linda Whitney, 1944–
    Walker Percy: A Comprehensive Descriptive Bibliography

First Printing: 1988

10 9 8 7 6 5 4 3 2 1

ISBN 0-917905-06-7

FAUST
PUBLISHING COMPANY

7523 Maple St. • New Orleans, La. 70118

For my daughter, Jane

Contents

Foreword

William Alexander Percy writes that as he went up to Sewanee to college, he was "innocent as an egg" about the workings of the world. The phrase has stayed in my mind as I have worked on this bibliography for the last 27 months, because soon into the project I knew that it described me, too, for a good part of that time.

When the project was suggested to me three years ago, I thought "That's easy. All it will take is hard work, and I've never been afraid of that." I remembered the various bibliographies I had compiled over the years, leading up to the twenty-odd pages of bibliography at the end of my dissertation. I could remember the rare pleasure of compiling a bibliography at the conclusion of a long, agonizing, sweaty, but ultimately rewarding bout of writing at the typewriter. The bibliography, I remembered, was the mindless thing one did after all the creativity, when one could smile slightly and think "I'm just too exhausted to do anything else," in a tone perhaps justifiably smug.

I did not know at all, however, what it was like to have the entire project be the compiling of a long list—no metaphors to play with, no revising at the kitchen table, no characters' motivations to investigate, no living writers to interview. Just the library, the indexes, the crypt-like microfilm room, the piles and piles of note cards—a kind of grotesque elephantiasis in one appendage of a research paper-gone-mad.

What I soon came to understand was that it is a short puff of expelled air that separates "corpus" from "corpse." The body of work seemed many days like an unwieldy corpse, of the sort John Cleese might secrete in a linen closet of his superficially respectable but truly absurd Fawlty Towers. He could hide the body, but he would never get completely rid of it. No matter what I did, the bibliography was always there, solid, uncommunicative, knowing its knowledge but not giving me a clue I did not have to pay handsomely for. I wrote 127

letters to editors of all the magazines, journals, and newspapers, here
and abroad, who had ever published anything on Percy. Their replies
would be a second check on my own findings if they could tell me
down to the shortest letter to the editor whether they had published
anything on Percy between 1980 and 1985. Many did not even bother
to return the self-addressed, stamped envelopes with a check in the
appropriate box. A few sent replies but never included their name or
publication. Many were gracious and helped me tremendously. A few
were outraged to be asked, thinking they were being asked to do my
primary research. "Look for yourself," they wrote indignantly.

What I did look at was pages and pages of fine-printed indexes,
often typed in computer codes that were nearly indeciferable. My eyes
ran in frustration at not being able to see the print, while my body
froze in the library air-conditioning cold enough to preserve any de-
composing corpse. I discovered slowly that if I didn't ask too much of
each day, the references would accumulate slowly, slowly, and things
began to be accomplished.

But the speed was agonizingly slow—like trying to see the hands
of a clock move or the petals of a flower open. You had to not concen-
trate too hard or you wouldn't see anything change. So I stopped
"casting ahead"—as Percy writes *Love in the Ruins*—to the end of the
research, I stopped imagining the victory or even getting to the typewriter and out of the library, and just did my scavenging, slowly,
slowly.

Soon I could see life in the thing. I felt as though I knew the
writers whose names would turn up again and again—the "old hands"
at Percy criticism became my oldest, long-lost friends. I saw a vast
web of community among all of us who had read and then written on
Walker Percy. I began to see politics afoot in the corpus, too. There
was the smug, New York reviewer—Cheever's Northeastern Man, the
most fortunate, undeprived American and ironically the most despair-
ing. Like any one of us, this reviewer had gone to Walker Percy—to
the very newest of his books—with a secret yearning to be told how to
live his life. And he had looked so hard or maybe had wanted such an
easy recipe—as easy as making one of "Cud'n Walker's Uncle Will's
Favorite Mint Juleps"—and had missed the point of Percy's hard
truths. And so the disappointed reviewer had written a snotty review,
full of smug, undergraduate word-games such as "The Trickle-Down
Theory of Uplift." I could see the despair of such a man, and recog-
nized it as my own.

On the other hand, I found loving reviewers whose intellectual
gratitude to Percy for being alive, for writing as he does, shines

through in every word they write; Tracy Kenyon Lisher's review of *The Second Coming,* which Carol Dana quotes in her excellent annotated bibliography of Percy's works, is one of these: "Percy's religious feelings are born in the nature of communication—'with words the human mind brings beauty out of hiding.' His characters long for a bond between themselves and reality. In this novel Will Barrett moves 'from absolute loneliness to re-discovery of commitment, from dread of catastrophe to hope of community.' "

Too, I found emotionally-charged debates between writers of reviews and their readers, who would fire off vituperative rebuttals of the ignominious stance the reviewer had taken earlier in the pages of the magazine or journal. These rebuttals fairly smoked with high dudgeon, and I could see that the readers had read Walker Percy's books as if their very lives depended on it (which, of course, in one important sense, they do). These exchanges took on a real-life, win-or-lose significance for me.

Finally, I found that the thoughtful scholars who wrote for the journals, their reviews often coming a healthy one or two years after the publication of one of Percy's books, aroused once more my curiosity to go back and read the novels yet another time. As J.P. Telotte writes in a review of Panthea Reid Broughton's fine edition of *The Art of Walker Percy,* Percy fulfills admirably the novelist's task of "touching the sore spot of our innermost afflictions." For, in so many ways, Dr. Percy "has sought to name those problems which constantly plague modern man and affirm our ability to bear with them." These words reminded me at the time of the last line of a short story by Frank Conroy: "What mattered was that everyone was connected in a web, that pain was part of the web, and yet despite it, people loved one another. That's what you found out when you got older."

Even the few reviewers who wrote negative reviews—such as Richard H. King in his *Virginia Quarterly Review* essay on *The Second Coming*—admit, sometimes grudgingly, that Percy has many strengths as a novelist: "First, he finds in the most prosaic life a serious philosophical or religious dimension. As a master analyst of everydayness, he has a nose for the authentic problems of the American middle classes—boredom, nameless anxiety, disconnection—yet he sturdily resists what he calls 'California' solutions . . . . Second, Percy can translate these existential situations into compelling fiction . . . . Third, Percy has a marvelous ear for language and eye for social nuance and detail."

However, most of the reviewers who have taken time to think about what they have read see the value of his work in an even more concrete way, as does Walter Sullivan, writing in the *Sewanee Review:* "Throughout his distinguished career, both as an essayist and a novelist, Percy has been concerned with the contradictions of modern man's existence: alienation, loss of freedom, spiritual misery for which no cause is readily discernible, inability to distinguish between what is make-believe and what is real. Percy's work badgers us with questions. 'Look, look,' his characters urge us. 'See what is around you. The first step toward salvation is to perceive that things have gone badly wrong.' "

All the writers listed here have looked at our predicament; they have seen that "things have gone badly wrong." As they have done, perhaps the place for any reader to look first is in the pages of Percy's novels, with his essays as glosses on the text. For such a willingness to read and to begin the search forms the living web of relationship which links all the Percy scholars and reviewers. In this way even a list—a bibliography—has a life to it, a subtle quickening that hints at the richness of life at the primary source.

Linda Whitney Hobson
New Orleans
April 20, 1987

Preface and Acknowledgements

At the beginning of my work on this bibliography, I found several standard guides helpful, such as Fredson Bowers' *Principles of Bibliographical Description* (Princeton, 1949), Philip Gaskell's *A New Introduction to Bibliography,* and Margaret Mann's *Introduction to Cataloguing and the Classification of Books.* After I read several other books of this type, and I could see them begin to repeat one another in my notes, I moved onto various descriptive bibliographies themselves, a study which was perhaps more valuable than the study of theory. I looked at many of the bibliographies published by Gale Research of Detroit, but found the Bruccoli-Clark bibliographies published by the University of Pittsburgh Press the most helpful of all.

I followed exclusively the documentation forms as set forth in the *MLA Handbook for Writers of Research Papers* (1984) and borrowed the following abbreviations from several of the standard bibliographies mentioned above:

[ ]	=	pages unnumbered but extrapolated from those which are numbered.
|	=	end of a line of print, a symbol used so as not to be confused with end marks of punctuation within the text.
CAPS	=	material typed in caps is illustrative of how it appears in the text.
[1–13]^{16}	=	example of a description of gatherings, showing how the book is sewn together. This book would have thirteen gatherings of 16 leaves.
TP/SI	=	New Orleans' main newspaper, *The Times-Picayune/The States-Item.*
rev.	=	review
rpt.	=	reprinted

LWH = copy examined in the personal library of Linda Whitney
        Hobson
WP = copy examined in the personal library of Walker Percy

Many people deserve special mention for their help with this project. In the summer of 1984, Dr. Walker Percy delivered to me a huge box of his own books for me to describe; I especially enjoyed seeing the books I've come to love so much in such languages as Japanese, Danish, or Portuguese. He followed up this kindness with many letters of encouragement. Rhoda Faust was also helpful, and would brook no nay-saying along the way, a discipline which (probably no surprise to her) eventually and surprisingly (to me) bore fruit. Herb Yellin, publisher of the Lord John Press, Northridge, California, wrote me several letters including technical information and cheering along the way.

Rebecca Malek and the Reference Librarians at the Howard-Tilton Memorial Library of Tulane University and the Reference Librarians at Loyola University in New Orleans were generous in their advice on problems of description and locating indexes. The following people also contributed to various sections of this work: Prof. Phinizy Spalding, Dept. of History, U. of Georgia; Miss Jennie P. Johnson, Assistant to Prof. Spalding in Athens; Christine Valentine, Editorial Director, The Franklin Library in New York City; Mary Jane Cone, Southern Educational Communications Association in Columbia, South Carolina; Peter Hayes, at Alfred A. Knopf, Inc. in New York; and especially Neil Kramer, Douglas Warshow and Mary-Alice Moore at Farrar, Straus & Giroux, Inc. who sent me a great deal of very helpful information. Prof. Claudia D. Johnson, of the English Department at The University of Alabama, Prof. Fred C. Hobson, Jr., of the English Department at Louisiana State University in Baton Rouge and Patrick Samway, S.J., of *America* magazine also advised this work.

Encouragement was also offered generously by my family as well as by my many friends in New Orleans, some of whom are affiliated with Newman School and Trinity Church. To all these people, let me express my gratitude for their kindness. Finally, I wish to thank my daughter, Jane, whose patience and tacit understanding gave me a great deal of time and strength for this task.

L.W.H.

WALKER PERCY'S STUDY, COVINGTON, LA., 1986

WALKER PERCY, BECHAC'S RESTAURANT, 1987

Introduction

It turned out to be a somewhat peculiar experience, "reading" this book—if that is what you do with a bibliography. Peculiar? Peculiar how? Peculiar in one sense of the ongoing effort of trying to connect up the person of the bibliographer, whom I know, with this awesome scholarly apparatus. I hasten to say there is no reason why a very bright, attractive young woman should not be a first-rate scholar. It's just that I've always associated bibliographies with old, dead Germans. This ignorant sentiment derives no doubt from my own fecklessness in the field. I can still remember the worst part of having to write a paper in a college English class or an article for a quarterly: the footnotes and the half-page bibliography at the end. Where to put semicolons? Italics? I can still remember the big fat red, sternly encircled, B-. Linda Hobson knows where to put everything.

Then there is the peculiarity of the feeling of conjoined gratitude and embarrassment—gratitude that Linda should have thought it worthwhile to undertake such a task, embarrassment at seeing one's own works. Actually there is a kind of shame in an author looking at his own work so compiled. One can only do it by sidelong glances. One doesn't like to be reminded that he might have done better here, didn't get it quite right there. It is not my favorite pastime. I'd rather watch "Barnaby Jones."

But in the end gratitude predominates. We are, after all, a tiny minority, we serious writers, readers, critics, reviewers—by "serious" I also mean comic, of course. I'd rather be attacked by Joyce Carol Oates than praised by Donahue. What else to do in a society which believes that Shirley MacLaine has discovered the Secret of Life and that Jane Fonda knows the secret of politics and health? What to do? One does not speak ill of fellow writers. What to say about them, then? They both have great legs.

How did I feel reading this? First, one experiences a queer shifting of gears. A novelist is not used to thinking of his novel as an actual book in hand, but rather as ghost stuff coming out of his head. But after all that is what one reads, books in hand. So I got to thinking about the mysterious connection between the two, the book in the writer's mind and the thing in the reader's hand. There is a connection. How can I not connect *The Brothers Karamazov* with the big fat Random House edition, fat as a bible, its pages slightly pulpy, crumbling at the corners and smelling like bread? Is this bad? And how can I disconnect Ivan and Mitya from reading about them sitting in a swing on my grandmother's porch in Athens, Georgia, in the 1930's? Should I?

What did I find least painful in considering this retrospect? I think I liked best the things most readers liked least—scenes in the novels when nothing much happened, like Binx Bolling walking home after work in Gentilly and looking at the evening sky—

—or peculiar encounters, such as slightly deranged Will Barrett falling out of a cave and into slightly deranged Allison's greenhouse. How do you fall out of a cave? I don't know, but I know when a love scene works, and this one works about as well as old Don Ameche meeting young Suzanne Somers by the boat rail in the moonlight on "Love Boat."

Another small pleasure is recollecting the semiotic sections of *The Message in the Bottle* and *Lost in the Cosmos*—chapters generally disliked by most readers. The pleasure derives from pointing out, like the smart-alec boy and the naked emperor, that most of the current theorists of language—structuralists, transformationalists, behaviorists, etc.—are up shit creek and can't get out without crawling over eight-year-old Helen Keller in North Alabama—

Such are the secret malices, perverse pleasures, devious designs upon the reader—herein faithfully catalogued.

—Walker Percy
Covington, Louisiana
October 21, 1987

Walker Percy:
A Comprehensive
Descriptive Bibliography

A. PRIMARY SOURCES

A.1.1. *The Moviegoer* (1961)

[i–x] [1–2] 3–241 [242–244]

[1–8]^{16}

Contents: pp. [i–ii]: blank; p. [iii]: half-title; p. [iv]: blank; p. [v]: title page; p. [vi]: copyright page: p. [vii]: dedication: 'In | Gratitude | To | W.A.P.'; p. [viii]: blank; p. [xi]: epigraph: '. . . the specific character of | despair is precisely this: it | is unaware of being despair.' | SØREN KIERKEGAARD, | *The Sickness Unto Death;* p. [x]: blank; p. 1: half-title; p. 2: blank; pp. 3–[242]: text, headed 'One'; p. [243] 'A NOTE ABOUT THE AU-THOR', dated *'March 1961';* p. [244]: 'A NOTE ON THE TYPE'.

Typography and paper: 8 ″ x 5$^{1}/_{4}$ ″; 33 lines per page; running heads: versos, 'THE *Moviegoer.*' Set in ELECTRA, 'a linotype face designed by the late W.A. Dwiggins (1880–1956).'

copy examined: The Louisiana Collection, Howard-Tilton Memorial Library, Tulane University, New Orleans.

Printing: Composed, printed, and bound by H. Wolff, New York.

A.1.1. *Publishing Information:* First edition published April, 1961; 1500 copies, $3.95, Alfred A. Knopf.

A.1.1.a. *The Moviegoer.* New York: Popular Library, 1962. Published simultaneously in Canada by McClelland and Stewart, Ltd.

A.1.1.b. _____. London: Eyre & Spottiswoode, 1963.

A.1.1.c. *Biografgaengeren.* Copenhagen: Gyldendal, 1964. Trans. by Knud Holst.

A.1.1.d. *The Moviegoer.* New York: Noonday Press, 1967. Published in Canada by Ambassador Books, Ltd., Rexdale, Ontario.

A.1.1.e. —————. New York: Avon, 1980.

A.1.1.f. Published in a limited edition in October, 1980, for subscribers to Franklin Library's Signed Editions series; set in 11-point Times Roman; printed on 60-pound Franklin Library Eggshell Wove (acidfree); illustrated by Walker Rane; bound in green leather, stamped with 22-karat gold, aeg; $45 per volume for subscribers; no retail sales; copies signed by the author.

A.1.1.g. *Der Kinogeher.* Frankfurt am Main: Suhrkamp Verlag, 1980. Trans. by Peter Handke.

A.1.1.h. *Biobesökaren.* Stockholm: P.A. Norstedt and Söners Förlag, 1980. Trans. by Staffan Holmgren.

A.1.1.i. *Le Cinéphile.* Paris: Pandora, 1982. Trans. by Claude Blanc.

A.1.1.j. *Mirajul Fericirii.* Bucharest: Editura Univers, 1982. Trans. by Cătălina-Antonia Stoenescu.

Farrar, Straus also negotiated contracts with these publishers to introduce foreign editions:

British: Secker and Warburg (May, 1977)
French: Editions Rivages (March, 1987)
Italian: Garzanti (February, 1963)
Japanese: Fuzambo (November, 1968)
Portuguese: Editora Globo (April, 1987)
Serbo Croatian: Zora of Zagreb (May, 1964)
Turkish: E. Yayinlari (December, 1971)

THE
MOVIEGOER

WALKER PERCY

Alfred A. Knopf   NEW YORK
1961

THE MOVIEGOER (1961), TITLE PAGE

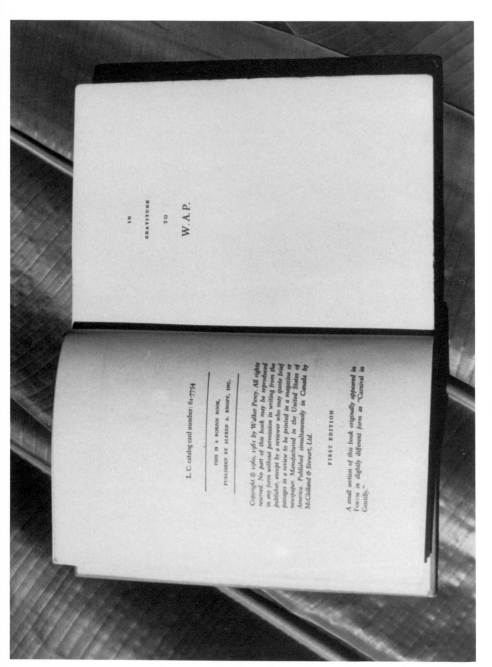

THE MOVIEGOER, COPYRIGHT AND DEDICATION PAGES

THE MOVIEGOER, DUST JACKET

A.1.2. *The Last Gentleman* (1966)

[i–vi] [1–2] 3–41 [42] 43–123 [124] 125–183 [184] 185–289 [290] 291–409

[1–13][16]

Contents: p. [i]: half-title; p. [ii]: *Also by Walker Percy* THE MOVIEGOER; p. [iii]: title page; p. [iv]: copyright page; p. [v]: Dedication 'FOR BUNT'; p. [vi]: epigraphs *'If a man cannot forget, he will never amount to much.' Søren Kierkegaard,* EITHER/OR | *'. . . We know now that the modern world is coming to an | end . . . at the same time, the unbeliever will emerge from | the fogs of secularism. He will cease to reap benefit from the | values and forces developed by the very Revelation he denies | . . . Loneliness in faith will be terrible. Love will disappear | from the face of the public world, but the more precious | will be that love which flows from one lonely person to an- | other . . . the world to come will be filled with animosity | and danger, but it will be a world open and clean. Romano Guardini,* THE END OF THE MODERN WORLD; p. [1] half-title; p. [2] Author's statement that characters and setting are fictional.

Typography and paper: 11/13 Baskerville; $5^{1}/_{2}''$ x $8^{1}/_{4}''$; 35 lines per page. Running heads at foot, 45 x 68 322M 50#.

Binding and Dust Jacket: material 3 pc. case-spine is Kennet 57180 green and sides are multicolor jet black; jacket 4 colors—black, blue, green, tan; endpapers Multicolor Spring Green.

copy examined: The Louisiana Collection, Howard-Tilton Memorial Library, Tulane University, New Orleans.

Printing: Composed, printed, and bound by H. Wolff, New York.

A.1.2. *Publishing Information:* First edition published 1966, 10,000 copies, $5.95, Farrar, Straus, & Giroux.

A.1.2.b. _____. London: Eyre & Spottiswoode, 1967.

A.1.2.c. _____. New York: Signet Books, New American Library, 1968.

A.1.2.d. _____. New York: Noonday, first printing, 1971, 1981. (Published simultaneously in Canada)

A.1.2.e. _____. Japan: S. Hamano, 1975. Trans. by Shigeo Hamano.

A.1.2.f. The Literary Guild also offered an edition to its members.

A.1.2.g. _____. London: Secker & Warburg, 1977.

Farrar, Straus also negotiated contracts with these publishers to introduce foreign editions:

French: Editions Rivages (March, 1987)
German: Suhrkamp (March, 1981)
Japanese: Fuzambo (November, 1968)

Also by Walker Percy
THE MOVIEGOER

Walker Percy

THE
LAST GENTLEMAN

FARRAR, STRAUS AND GIROUX / New York

For Margaret and Dick
with best wishes

From Walker

Walker Percy
Jan 14, 1966

THE LAST GENTLEMAN (1966), TITLE PAGE

THE LAST GENTLEMAN, COPYRIGHT PAGE

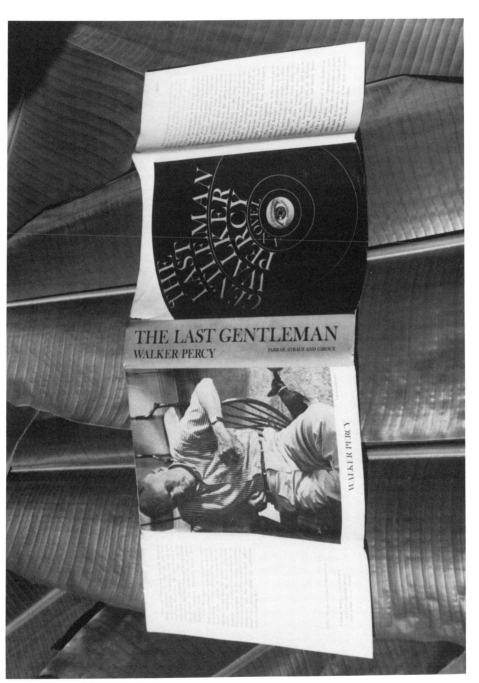

A.1.3. *Love in the Ruins* (1971)

[i–viii] [1–2] 3–58 [59–60] 61–170 [171–172] 173–191 [192–194] 195–242 [243–244] 245–377 [378–380] 381–403 [404–409]

[1–13]¹⁶

Contents: p. [i]: blank; p. [ii]: other titles by author; p. [iii]: half-title; pp. [iv–v]: title pages (see illustration); p. [vi]: copyright page; p. [vii]: dedication 'For SHELBY FOOTE'; p. [viii]: blank; p. [1]: 'JULY FOURTH'; p. [2]: blank; pp. 3–403: text, headed 'In a pine grove on the | southwest cusp on the interstate cloverleaf | 5 P.M./JULY 4' |

Typography and paper: 10/13/23¹/₂ Electra. 5¹/₂ " x 8¹/₄ "; 35 lines per page. Running feet: book title in cursive Clc (versos): chapter title (part) (rectos). Paper: Glatfelter 45 x 68, 345M 55#.

Binding and Dust Jacket: 1 pc. Fictionette RNV3750— black; bendpapers multicolor burnt orange; jacket 4 color—red, yellow, blue, copy examined: LWH

Printing: H. Wolff Book Manufacturing Co., New York

A.1.3. *Publishing Information:* First edition published 1971, 25,000 copies, $7.95, Farrar, Straus, & Giroux.

A.1.3.a. _____. London: Eyre & Spottiswoode, Ltd., 1971.

A.1.3.b. *Amore nas Ruínas*. Brazil, 1973.

A.1.3.c. *Amore tra le rovine: avventure di un cattivo cattolico mentre si avvicina la fine del mondo*. Milan: Rizzoli Editore, 1973. Trans. by Bruno Oddera.

A.1.3.d. *Amor nas Ruínas*. São Cristovão, Brazil: Editora Artenova, S.A., 1974. Trans. by Luis Corcão.

A.1.3.e. *Liebe in Ruinen: die Abenteuer eines schlechten Katholicken kurz vor dem Ende der Welt*. Frankfurt am Main: Suhrkamp, 1974.

A.1.3.f. *Love in the Ruins*. Tokyo: A.M. Heath and Co., Ltd. through Japan UNI Agency, Inc., 1976. Trans. by Yoshie Itabashi.

A.1.3.g. _____. London: Secker & Warburg, 1978.

A.1.3.h. The Book-of-the-Month Club also offered an edition to its
members.

Farrar, Straus also negotiated contracts with these publishers to introduce foreign editions:

Dutch: Uitgeverij de Fontein (November 1971)
French: Calmann-Levy (August, 1971)
Japanese: Kodansha (April, 1972)
Swedish: Norstedt (May, 1971)
Norstedt paperback (March, 1981)

LOVE IN THE RUINS (1971), COPYRIGHT PAGE

WALKER PERCY

LOVE IN THE RUINS

The Adventures of a Bad Catholic

at a Time Near the End of the World

Farrar, Straus & Giroux / NEW YORK

Walker Percy

Love in the Ruins
Walker Percy

Farrar Straus Giroux

A.1.4. *The Message in the Bottle* (1975)

[one leaf unnumbered] [i–ix] x [1–2] [3]–327 [328–331]
332–335 [336–340]

[1–11][16]

Contents: first leaf unnumbered; p. [i]: half-title; p. [ii]:
list of author's books; p. [iii]: title page; p. [iv]: copyright
page; p. [v]: dedication '*For* MARY PRATT *and* ANN';
p. [vi]: blank; p. [vii]: 'AUTHOR'S NOTE'; p. [viii]:
blank; p. [ix]: 'CONTENTS'; p. x: continuation of table
of contents; p. [1]: half-title; p. [2]: blank; p. [3]–327:
text, headed '1'; p. [328]: blank; p. [329]: 'BIBLIOGRA-
PHY'; p. [330]: blank; p. [331]–35: bibliography; pp.
[336–40]: blank.

Typography and paper: 10/13 x 23 Electra; $5^3/8''$ x $8^1/4''$;
36 lines per page; running heads: recto, title of essay;
verso, 'THE MESSAGE IN THE BOTTLE': paper $34''$
rolls 370/1$''$, 55#.

Binding and Dust Jacket: 1 pc. case, Vail Ballou stock
Natural finish no. 512 orange; endpapers plain white;
jacket in three colors—black, red, and yellow.

copy examined: LWH

Printing: name of printer not given in publisher's specs.

A.1.4. *Publishing Information:* First edition published 1975,
10,000 copies, $8.95, Farrar, Straus, & Giroux.

Book includes the following essays, all of which appeared
elsewhere first: "The Delta Factor," "The Loss of the
Creature," "Metaphor as Mistake," "The Man on the
Train," "Notes for a Novel about the End of the World,"
"The Message in the Bottle," "The Mystery of Lan-
guage," "Toward a Triadic Theory of Meaning," "The
Symbolic Structure of Interpersonal Process," "Culture:
The Antinomy of the Scientific Method," "Semiotic and a
Theory of Knowledge," "Symbol, Consciousness, and In-
tersubjectivity," "Symbol as Hermeneutic in Existential-
ism," "Symbol as Need," and "A Theory of Language."

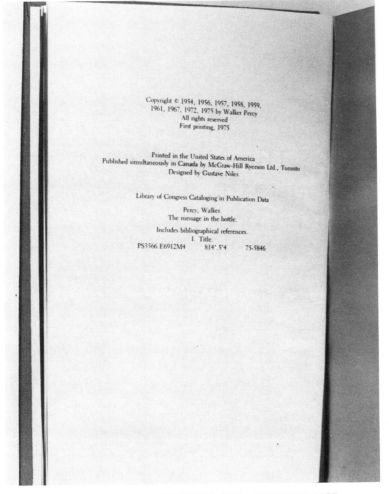

Printed in the United States of America
Published simultaneously in Canada by McGraw-Hill Ryerson Ltd., Toronto
Designed by Gustave Niles

Library of Congress Cataloging in Publication Data

Percy, Walker.
The message in the bottle.

Includes bibliographical references.
I. Title.
PS3566.E6912M4   814'.5'4   75-5846

THE MESSAGE IN THE BOTTLE (1975), COPYRIGHT PAGE

Walker Percy

THE MESSAGE
IN THE BOTTLE

How Queer Man Is, How Queer Language Is,

and What One Has to Do with the Other

FARRAR, STRAUS AND GIROUX

NEW YORK

THE MESSAGE IN THE BOTTLE, TITLE PAGE

THE MESSAGE IN THE BOTTLE, DUST JACKET

Walker Percy

The Message in the Bottle

How Queer Man Is,
How Queer Language Is, and
What One Has to Do with the Other

Walker Percy
The Message in the Bottle

Novels by WALKER PERCY

LOVE IN THE RUINS

"Walker Percy's third novel confirms once and for all what his first two had strongly suggested: there is not a better comic writer around. That *Love in the Ruins* is also a deeply pained protest against modern vulgarity in all its forms, and a moving expression of caution hope, gives breadth and power to the novel and emphasizes the persistent seriousness of its comedy."

JONATHAN YARDLEY

THE LAST GENTLEMAN

"A novel of the first rank that defies easy classification."

DENIS DONOGHUE

"A distinguished work of art . . . It succeeds brilliantly in dramatizing the contradictory nature of reality through characters who are at once typical of our condition yet wildly individual."

PETER BUITENHUIS

THE MOVIEGOER

"*The Moviegoer*, an intimation rather than a statement of mortality and the inevitability of that condition, is a truthful novel with shocks of recognitions and spasms of nostalgia for every—or nearly every—American. Mr. Percy, with compassion and without sentimentality or the maudlin irony of the cliché, examines the delusions and hallucinations, the daydreams and the dreams that afflict those who abstain from the customary ways of making do."

LEWIS GANNETT, HERBERT GOLD, JEAN STAFFORD. JUDGES, 1962 NATIONAL BOOK AWARD FOR FICTION

(continued from front flap)

in the life of Helen Keller on another summer day in Alabama in 1887.

He points out that since "language is part of man's singularity, symbolization may be an essential act of the mind. In a period when most psychology textbooks omit the word "symbol" he discusses the relations of symbol and meaning to "sum" against modern vulgarity in all its forms, and a moving expression of caution hope. "The Symbolic Structure of Interpretation," "The Symbolic Structure of Interpretation," "Consciousness, and Intersubjectivity," "The Symbolic Structure of Interpretation," "Semiotic and Process," and "Semiotic as Need."

Like castaways, we are waiting for the message in the bottle which will rescue us from the sadness that afflicts twentieth-century man. One suggestion in Mr. Percy's brilliant concluding essay, "A Theory of Language," is that Charles Peirce's theories of abduction perhaps provides the necessary clue in forming a theory of language (and therefore of man) that makes sense for what the author calls "the new post-modern age."

Jacket design by Janet Halverson

FARRAR STRAUS AND GIROUX
19 Union Square West
New York 10003

(continued on back flap)

For many years Walker Percy has been writing for little-known magazines about language and meaning and existence. "We return almost over the years," he writes, "has been the nature of human communication and, in particular, the consequence of man's unique discovery of the symbol." These writings, now brought together for the first time, make *The Message in the Bottle* a provocative and important book.

The theme of Mr. Percy's first book of nonfiction is summed up in his subtitle, *How Queer Man Is, How Queer Language Is, and What One Has to Do with the Other*. Mr. Percy, in addition to being a distinguished novelist, is a scientist who took his M.D. at Columbia and interned in pathology at Bellevue Hospital. He reveals how he discovered the Delta Factor—his term for man's breakthrough into the delight of language—"at a consciousness one summer day in Louisiana" and sets out thinking about an event in the 1950's thinking about an event

Walker Percy

The Message in the Bottle

A.1.5. *Lancelot* (1977)

[i–x] [1–2] 3–6 [7–8] 9–37 [38–40] 41–67 [68–70] 71–102 [103–104] 105–131 [132–134] 135–160 [161–162] 163–182 [183–184] 185–246 [247–248] 249–257 [258–262]

[1–4]^{16} [5]^{8} [6–9]^{16}

Contents: p. [i]: half-title; p. [ii]: blank; p. [iii]: other books by the author; p. [iv]: blank; p. [v]: title page; p. [vi]: copyright page; p. [vii]: four lines from Dante's *The Divine Comedy,* in Italian and English; p. [viii]: blank; p. [ix]: author's explanation of fictionality of his characters and setting; p. [x]: blank; p. [1]: titled '1'; p. [2]: blank; pp. 3–257: text; pp. [258–262]: blank.

Typography and paper: Set in VIP 10/14 Palatino; 32 lines per page, no running heads; $5^{1}/_{2}$ " x $8^{1}/_{4}$ ", paper 34 " roll Penn Book Nat. Vellum 55# 360/1 ".

Binding and Dust Jacket: 1 pc. case, Vail Ballou cloth 512 Natural Finish (orange-red); 3 color jacket—black, red, and yellow.

copy examined: LWH

Printing: Vail-Ballou Press, Inc.

A.1.5. *Publishing Information:* First edition published 1977, 30,000 copies, $8.95, Farrar, Straus, & Giroux.

A.1.5.a. _____. New York: Book-of-the-Month Club, 1977. Limited edition. Gilt and red leather, boxed.

A.1.5.b. _____. London: Secker & Warburg, 1977.

A.1.5.c. _____. Stockholm: P.A. Norstedt & Söners Förlag, 1978. Trans. by Caj Lundgren.

A.1.5.d. *La Confesión de Lancelot.* Barcelona, Buenos Aires, México: Ediciones Grijalbo, S.A., 1978. Trans. by Manuel Bartolomé.

A.1.5.e. *Lancelot.* München/Zürich: Droemersche Verlaganstalt Th. Knaur Nachf., 1978. Trans. by Gisela Stege.

A.1.5.f. _____. Droemer Knaur, for the German Book-Partnership of C.A. Koch Publishers: Berlin, Darmstadt, and Vienna, and two other publishers in Stuttgart and Vienna, 1978. Jacket design by Jürgen Richter.

Copyright © 1977 by Walker Percy
All rights reserved
First printing, 1977
Printed in the United States of America
Published simultaneously in Canada by McGraw-Hill Ryerson Ltd., Toronto
Designed by Jacqueline Schuman

Library of Congress Cataloging in Publication Data

Percy, Walker
Lancelot

I. Title
PZ4.P4311SLan   [PS3566.E6912]   813'.54   76-57197

LANCELOT, COPYRIGHT PAGE

LANCELOT (1977), TITLE PAGE

LANCELOT, DUST JACKET

GOING BACK TO GEORGIA

by Walker Percy

[handwritten inscription]

THE FERDINAND PHINIZY LECTURES
The University of Georgia
Copyright 1978

GOING BACK TO GEORGIA, TITLE AND COPYRIGHT PAGE

GOING BACK TO GEORGIA (1978), COVER

Farrar, Straus also negotiated contracts with the following publishers to introduce foreign editions:

Norwegian: Aschehoug (May, 1977)

Hungarian: Europa (March, 1984)

A.1.6. *Going Back to Georgia* (1978)

[i–iv] v [vi] vii [viii] ix [x] 1–18

[1][14]

Contents: p. [i]: half-title; p. [ii]: blank; p. [iii]: title; p. [iv]: blank; p. v: CONTENTS; p. [vi]: blank; p. vii: FOREWORD, George O. Marshall, Jr., | *Professor of English* | The University of Georgia; p. [viii]: blank; p. ix: INTRODUCTION, B. Phinizy Spalding, *Chairman* | Ferdinand Phinizy Lectureship Committee | The University of Georgia

Typography and paper: $5^1/2''$ x $8^1/2''$; Palatino typeface; Classic Laid White text paper.

Binding: India cream cover with brown ink, paper.

copy examined: WP

Printing: published under the imprint of the Ferdinand Phinizy Lectures

Publishing Information: 500 copies, first printing, not for sale, 'but were distributed gratis to the University of Georgia Foundation Trustees (the Phinizy Lectureship series is funded within this organization); to various college presidents throughout the South; to outstanding members of the University of Georgia Alumni Association; and to members of the Phinizy family (of which Percy is himself one).' 250 copies, second printing. Rpt. *The Georgia Review,* 32 (1978): 499–511, in slightly different form. Rpt. *Harper's,* 258 (1979): 72–83.

QUESTIONS
they never
asked
me

WALKER PERCY

1979

LORD JOHN PRESS: NORTHRIDGE, CALIFORNIA

SAME EDITION
"O" MADE INTO "Q" BY HAND ON SOME COPIES

QUESTIONS
they never
asked
me

WALKER PERCY

1979

LORD JOHN PRESS: NORTHRIDGE, CALIFORNIA

QUESTIONS THEY NEVER ASKED ME (1979), TITLE PAGE
"O" PRINTED BY MISTAKE INSTEAD OF "Q"

A.1.7. *Questions They Never Asked Me* (1979)

[i–vi] 1–39 [40–42]

[1–3]⁸

Contents: pp. [i–ii]: blank; p. [iii]: half-title; p. [iv]: blank; p. [v]: title; p. [vi]: copyright; pp. 1–39: text; p. [40]: colophon page: 'This first edition of *Questions They Never Asked Me* | is limited to three hundred numbered copies and fifty | deluxe copies specially bound, all of which have been | signed by the author. | The paper is Frankfurt mouldmade and the type is | Aldus. | Designed and printed by Grant Dahlstrom for the | Lord John Press. | This is a presentation copy (Signature)'; pp. [41–42]: blank.

Typography and paper: Set in Aldus; 5¹/₄" x 7¹/₄", 28 lines per page; Frankfurt mouldmade paper with horizontal chain lines.

Binding: limited edition, signed, has linen spine with paper boards, turquoise linen with turquoise and light blue design; deluxe edition, signed, in full blue leather, gold stamped on spine.

copies examined: limited edition, LWH; deluxe edition, WP

Printing: Designed and printed by Grant Dahlstrom for the Lord John Press, Northridge, CA.

A.1.7. *Publishing Information:* First edition published 8 February 1980. 300 copies in first printing, 33 presentation copies: $35. 50 copies, deluxe: $75. The Lord John Press, 19073 Los Alimos Street, Northridge, California 91326.

Note: An issue point on the title page exists on an unknown number of copies subsequently corrected by hand. The letter "Q" had the slash missing, looking like "O."

QUESTIONS THEY NEVER ASKED ME, COPYRIGHT PAGE

BOURBON WALKER PERCY

Esto nil desideraes se nil impetidum memor
—HORTHANUS

PALAEMON PRESS LIMITED

BOURBON (1981), TITLE PAGE

A.1.8. *Bourbon* (1975, 1979)

[i–vi] [1–9] [10–14]

[1]^{10}

Contents: p. [i]: blank; p. [ii]: blank; p. [iii]: half-title; p. [iv]: blank; p. [v]: title page; p. [vi]: copyright page: '*Bourbon* Copyright 1975, 1979 by Walker Percy | This essay first appeared in *Esquire,* December 1975'; p. [11]: 'This first edition of | BOURBON | is limited to two hundred and thirty copies. | Two hundred copies, numbered 1–200, are | for public sale; thirty copies, *hors commerce,* and | numbered i–xxx, are for distribution by the author and | publisher. All copies are signed by the author. This is copy | xxviii' (handwritten in red ink) (signature follows); p. [12]: 'Printed by Heritage Printers, Inc.'

Chapbook, 5$^1/_2$ " x 6$^3/_4$ ".

copy examined: WP

Publishing Information: First limited, signed edition. Published July, 1979, at $20.00.

A.1.8.a. *Bourbon* (1981)

[i–vi] [1–8] [9–14]

[1]^{10}

Contents: pp. [i–ii]: blank; p. [iii]: title; p. [iv]: copyright: '*Bourbon* Copyright 1975, 1979, 1981, by Walker Percy | This essay first appeared in Esquire, December 1975.' p. [v]: dedication: 'To S.M.' p. [vi]: blank; pp. [1–8]: text; p. [8] Postscript: 'Cud'n Walker's Uncle Will's Favorite Mint Julep Receipt'; pp. [9–10]: blank; p. [11]: 'This edition is limited to 150 copies | AUTHOR'S COPY (In pencil, all caps) (Signature)

Limited edition, 6$^1/_8$ " x 9$^7/_8$ ", watermark "Arches" written vertically in lower right corner each leaf.

copy examined: WP

Publishing Information: Second limited, signed edition. Published May, 1981, at $60.00. Fewer than 100 copies of the second edition were bound. Twenty-six of these were lettered A–Z, for distribution by the author and publisher. The other bound copies were numbered in red below the

BOURBON, COPYRIGHT PAGE

printed statement above. Published by Palaemon Press, Winston-Salem, N.C.

A.1.9. *The Second Coming* (1980)

[i–vi] [1–2] 3–229 [230–232] 233–259 [360] [361–62]

$[1–6]^{16}$ $[7]^{8}$ $[8–12]^{16}$

Contents: p. [i]: half-title; p. [ii]: blank; p. [iii]: other titles by author; p. [iv]: blank; p. [v]: title; p. [vi]: copyright page; p. [1]: 'PART ONE'; p. [2]: blank; pp. 3–229: text; p. [230]: blank; p. [231]: 'PART TWO'; p. [232]: blank; p. 233–[360]: text; p. [361–362]: blank.

Typography and paper: 10 on 12 Janson; $5^{1}/_{2}''$ x $8^{1}/_{4}''$; 39 lines per full text page, no running heads; paper 55# Cream White 350/1".

Binding and Dust Jacket: 1 pc. case Kennett 66090; endpapers Rainbow Cafe TA; jacket 4 colors—gold, black, orange, and yellow.

copy examined: LWH—FSG edition; WP—Franklin Library edition.

Printing: Maryland Linotype Composition Co. 2315 Hollins St. Baltimore, MD 21223, for Farrar, Straus, & Giroux.

A.1.9. *Publishing Information:* First edition published 27 June 1980 for subscribers to The Franklin Library's First Edition Society. Set in 10-point Baskerville; printed on 60# Franklin Library Smooth White (acidfree) paper; illustrated by Steven H. Stroud; bound in olive-green leather, stamped with 22-karat gold, aeg; $45 per volume for subscribers; no retail sales.

copy examined: WP, includes 'A limited edition of 450 numbered copies, signed by the author, was privately printed. (Signature)' The Franklin Library, 800 Third Avenue, New York, NY 10022.

A.1.9.a. _____. First printing (book described above) 1980, 30,000 copies, $12.95. New York: Farrar, Straus, & Giroux.

A.1.9.b. _____. Published simultaneously in Canada by McGraw-Hill Ryerson Ltd., Toronto, 1980.

A.1.9.c. _____. London: Secker & Warburg, 1981.

A.1.9.d. *De Yttersta Dagarna.* Stockholm: P.A. Norstedt & Söners Förlag, 1984. Trans. by Staffan Holmgren.

A.1.9.e. *Le Signes de l'Apocalypse.* Paris: Calmann-Lévy, 1982. Trans. by F. et G. Casari.

Farrar, Straus also negotiated contracts with these publishers to introduce foreign editions:

German: Suhrkamp (March, 1981)

Portuguese: Francisco Alves Editores (April, 1981)

THE SECOND COMING, COPYRIGHT PAGE

THE SECOND COMING

WALKER PERCY

FARRAR · STRAUS · GIROUX · New York

THE SECOND COMING (1980), TITLE PAGE

THE SECOND COMING, DUST JACKET

A.1.10. *Lost in the Cosmos* (1983)

[i–viii] [1]–262 [263–264]

[1]^{10} [2–4]^{16} [5–6]^{14} [7]^{10} [8]^{16} [9–11]^8

Contents: p. [i]: half-title; p. [ii]: list of 7 works by author to 1983; p. [iii]: title; p. [iv]: copyright; p. [v]: dedication: *'For my fellow space travelers,* | *John Walker, Robert, David, Jack';* p. [vi]: blank; p. [vii]: epigraph: 'We are unknown, we knowers, to ourselves . . . Of necessity | we remain strangers to our selves, we understand ourselves | not, in ourselves we are bound to be mistaken, for each of us | holds good to all eternity the motto, "Each is the farthest | away from himself"—as far as ourselves are concerned we are | not knowers. | Nietzsche'; p. [vii]: blank; pp. [1]–262: text; pp. [263–264]: blank.

Typography and paper: Set in 11 on 14 Janson x24 picas; 34 lines per page, running heads: rectos, chapter titles: versos, 'LOST IN THE COSMOS'; 5^1/$_2$″ x 8^1/$_4$″, paper 22^1/$_2$″ rolls Sebago 55#.

Binding and Dust Jacket: material No. 512 Black natural finish extending 1″ onto No. 201 Smoke; 4 color jacket— orange, tan, silver, black.

copy examined: LWH

Printing: Maryland Linotype Composition Co., Inc., 2315 Hollins Street, Baltimore, MD 21223.

A.1.10. *Publishing Information:* First edition published 1983. 35,000 copies, $14.95, Farrar, Straus, & Giroux.

A.1.10.a. _____. Published simultaneously in Canada. Toronto: McGraw-Hill Ryerson, Ltd., 1983.

By Walker Percy

NOVELS

The Moviegoer
The Last Gentleman
Love in the Ruins
Lancelot
The Second Coming

NON-FICTION

The Message in the Bottle
Lost in the Cosmos

Walker Percy

LOST
IN
THE
COSMOS

The Last Self-Help Book

Farrar, Straus & Giroux
NEW YORK

First printing, 1983

Printed in the United States of America

Published simultaneously in Canada by
McGraw-Hill Ryerson Ltd., Toronto

Designed by Tere LoPrete

Library of Congress Cataloging in Publication Data

Percy, Walker.
  Lost in the cosmos.

I. Title.
PS3566.E6912L6   1983   818'.5407   83-1590

LOST IN THE COSMOS, COPYRIGHT PAGE

LOST IN THE COSMOS, DUST JACKET

A.1.11. *How to Be an American Novelist in Spite of Being Southern And Catholic* (1982, 1984)

This volume comprises The Flora Levy Lecture in the Humanities, 1982; printed by The University of Southwestern Louisiana Printing Services, Lafayette, Louisiana, 1984. The lecture is Volume 3 in the series.

Includes a preface by Prof. Maurice duQuesnay and an introduction by Prof. Panthea Reid Broughton.

Jacket displays a reproduction of "W. Percy: A Novelist in Spite of Himself," oil portrait by George Rodrigue.

500 published, $3.50 each.

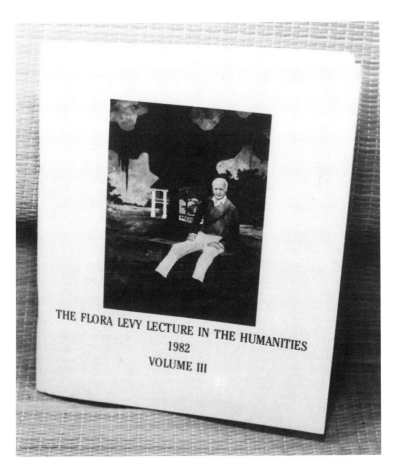

HOW TO BE AN AMERICAN NOVELIST . . . (1982, 1984), COVER

The Flora Levy Lecture in the Humanities

1982

How To Be

An American Novelist

In Spite of Being

Southern and Catholic

Walker Percy

The University of Southwestern Louisiana

Lafayette, Louisiana

HOW TO BE AN AMERICAN NOVELIST . . . , TITLE PAGE

HOW TO BE AN AMERICAN NOVELIST . . . , COPYRIGHT PAGE

FOREIGN EDITIONS OF SOME OF PERCY'S BOOKS

The City of the Dead

THE CITY OF THE DEAD (1985)

A.1.12. *The City of the Dead* (February, 1985)

Walker Percy; illustrated by Lyn Hill.

Broadside, 20 " x 22 " published by Lord John Press, Northridge, California.

Arches paper; printed by lithography in color.

Published, February 1985; signed by Walker Percy and Lyn Hill; 100 numbered copies and 26 lettered copies (A-Z); 25 presentation copies, so stated.

Retail price: $75.00; lettered copies: $125.00.

A.1.13. *Diagnosing the Modern Malaise* (October, 1985)

[i–viii] 1–22 [23–24]

[1–2]^8

Contents: pp. [i–ii]: blank; p. [iii]: half-title; p. [iv]: photo of author; p. [v]: author's name, both printed and signed; p. [vi]: blank; p. [vii]: title page; p. [viii]: copyright page.

Typography and paper: Times Roman type; Strathmore Pastelle Text Paper, 16 pages, 6 ″ x 9 ″.

Binding: 250 copies bound in grey cloth with photos of Percy on the cover. 50 copies bound in $^1/_4$ leather and red cloth (pictures of Percy on the cover), gold line stamped on front.

Copy examined: Rhoda K. Faust

Printing: limited signed edition, designed and printed by Herb Yellin and Carl Bennitt.

Publishing Information: 250 numbered copies, 50 deluxe copies, 25 presentation copies. $50.00 regular edition; $125.00 deluxe edition. Faust Publishing, 7523 Maple Street, New Orleans, LA 70118.

DIAGNOSING THE MODERN MALAISE, COVER,
DELUXE SIGNED LIMITED EDITION

DIAGNOSING THE MODERN MALAISE (1985), COVER, SIGNED LIMITED EDITION

Copyright © 1985 by Walker Percy

Faust Publishing
7523 Maple Street
New Orleans, LA 70118

ISBN 0-917905-02-4

DIAGNOSING THE MODERN MALAISE

by

Walker Percy

FAUST PUBLISHING 1985
NEW ORLEANS, LOUISIANA

The first edition of
Novel-Writing in an Apocalyptic Time
is limited to three hundred numbered copies
and one hundred deluxe copies specially bound,
all of which have been signed by the authors.

The type is Cheltenham and the paper Rives buff.

Designed and printed by Herb Yellin and
Carl Bennitt for Faust Publishing.
Binding by Marianna Blau.

This is number 17 of 100.

Faust Publishing
7523 Maple Street
New Orleans, LA 70118

ISBN: 0-917905-01-6

A.1.14. *Novel Writing in an Apocalyptic Time* (October, 1986)

[i–xii] 1–28 [29–32]

[1–2]⁸ [3]⁶

Contents: p. [i]: half-title; p. [ii]: blank; p. [iii]: half-title; p. [iv]: blank; p. [v]: title page; p. [vi]: copyright page; p. [vii]: photo of Percy; p. [viii]: blank; p. [ix]: Introductory Remarks by Percy on the occasion of the inauguration of the Eudora Welty Chair of Southern Studies at Millsaps College; p. [x]: blank; p. [xi]: half-title; p. [xii]: blank; pp. 1–23: Percy's address; p. [24]: photo of Eudora Welty; p. 25–28: Eudora Welty's Afterword; pp. [29–30]: blank; p. [31]: colophon page; p. [32]: blank.

Typography and paper: Cheltenham type; Rives buff paper, 44 pages, 6 " x 9 ".

Binding: 300 numbered copies bound in grey cloth with dark red printing on spine and cover, including a postmodernist, curving, spiderweb-like design.

Copy examined: LWH

Printing: 300 numbered copies and 100 deluxe copies specially bound, all of which have been signed by the authors. Designed and printed by Herb Yellin and Carl Bennitt for Faust Publishing. Binding by Marianna Blau. Faust Publishing, 7523 Maple Street, New Orleans, LA 70118.

Walker Percy

Novel Writing in an

Apocalyptic Time

with an
Afterword
by
Eudora Welty

Faust Publishing 1986
New Orleans, Louisiana

NOVEL WRITING IN AN APOCALYPTIC TIME, TITLE PAGE

NOVEL WRITING IN AN APOCALYPTIC TIME, COVERS, SIGNED LIMITED EDITION AND DELUXE SIGNED LIMITED EDITION

A.1.15. *The Thanatos Syndrome* (1987)

[i-vii] viii [1–3] 4–64 [65] 66–131 [132–33] 134–262 [263] 264–323 [324–25] 326–72

[1]^8 [2]^{16} [3]^8 [4–5]^{16} [6]^8 [7–12]^{16} [13]^{24}

Contents: p. [i.]: half-title; p. [ii]: blank; p. [iii]: title page; p. [iv]: copyright page; p. [v]: Dedication *'To Robert Coles';* p. [vi]: blank; pp. [vii]–[viii]: Introduction, all in italics; p. [1]: half-title; p. [2]: blank; pp. [3]–64: Part I; pp. [65]–131: Part II; p. [132]: blank; pp. [133]–262: Part III; pp. [263]–323: Part IV; p. [324]: blank; p. [325]–372: Part V.

Typography and paper: $^{11}/_{13}$ Linotype Janson, and Janson italic. 6^1/$_8$″ x 9^1/$_4$″; 40 lines per page. Running heads: left, author's name in 11 pt. Janson C & CS machine; right, book title in 11 pt. Janson ital. c & lc. Paper: 50# Antique cream 396 ppi.

Binding and Dust Jacket: 3-pc. case; spine color: Black Kennett #19990; side color: Rainbow Colonial Jade; endpapers white to match text. Dust jacket: 4-color process in black, gray, jade, white, pink, yellow.

copy examined: LWH

Printing: R. R. Donnelley & Sons
Harrisonburg, VA

A.1.15. *Publishing Information:* First edition published March, 1987. 59,000 copies printed, of which 1,500 went to Book-of-the-Month Club for its Dual Main Selection, and 250 for a limited edition. Second printing: 15,000 copies; third printing: 7,000 copies; fourth printing, 2,500 copies. $17.95. Farrar, Straus & Giroux. Distributed in Canada.

A.1.15.a. _____. London: Andre Deutsch, 1987.

A.1.15.b. Paperback sale to Fawcett Books: 2 printings sold out, as of July 21, 1987.

A.1.15.c. Quality Paperback Book Club, Book-of-the-Month Club, Inc. 485 Lexington Avenue, New York, NY 10017. Used original FSG plates and cover for large-sized edition like old Scribner paperbacks. 1987.

Farrar, Straus also negotiated contracts with these publishers to introduce foreign editions:

> Danish: Kay Holkenfeldt (April, 1987)
> Dutch: Het Spectrum (February, 1987)
> French: Editions Rivage (March, 1987)
> German: Hanser (March, 1987)
> Italian: Feltrinelli (March, 1987)
> Swedish: Norstedt (April, 1987)

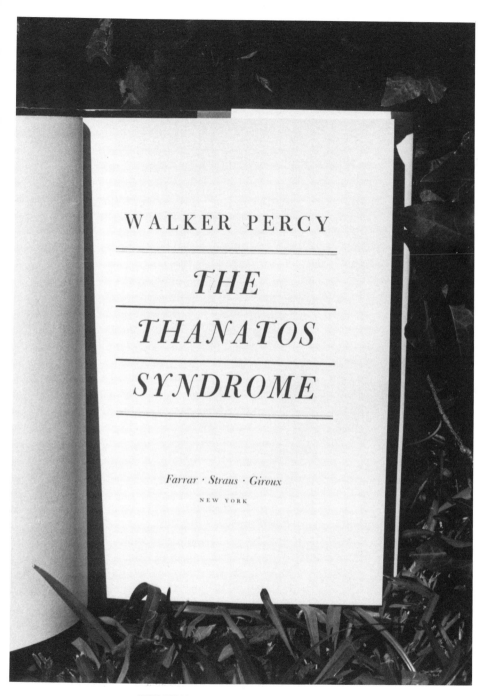

WALKER PERCY

THE

THANATOS

SYNDROME

Farrar · Straus · Giroux

NEW YORK

THE THANATOS SYNDROME (1987), TITLE PAGE

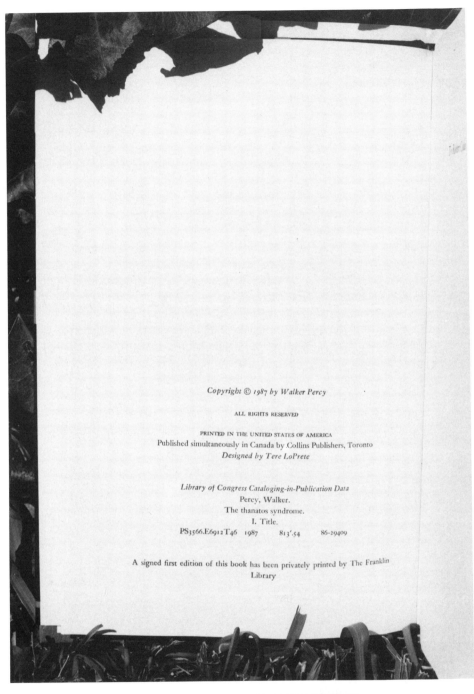

Copyright © 1987 by Walker Percy

ALL RIGHTS RESERVED

PRINTED IN THE UNITED STATES OF AMERICA
Published simultaneously in Canada by Collins Publishers, Toronto
Designed by Tere LoPrete

Library of Congress Cataloging-in-Publication Data
Percy, Walker.
The thanatos syndrome.
I. Title.
PS3566.E6912T46 1987   813'.54   86-29409

A signed first edition of this book has been privately printed by The Franklin
Library

THE THANATOS SYNDROME, COPYRIGHT PAGE

THE THANATOS SYNDROME, DUST JACKET

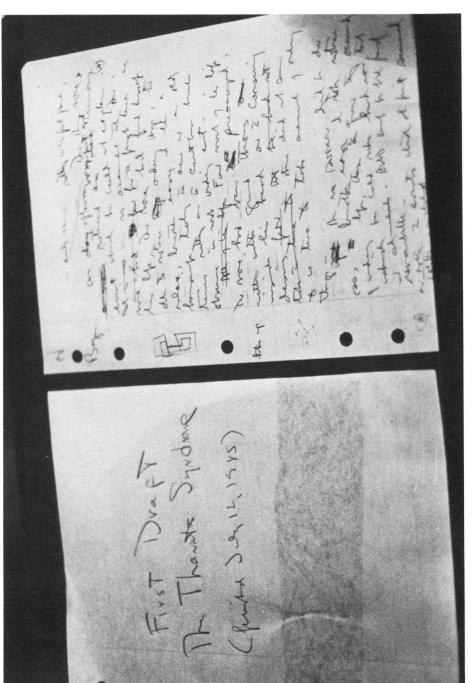

THE THANATOS SYNDROME, FIRST PAGE OF THE FIRST DRAFT

THE THANATOS SYNDROME, TYPED MANUSCRIPT-IN-PROGRESS

A.2. Periodicals: Reviews and review essays (chronological)

"Reviewing the Books." Rev. of *This Was Ivor Trent*, by Claude Houghton. *Carolina Magazine* 64 (Feb. 1935): 28.

"Reviewing the Books." Rev. of *Francis the First*, by Francis Hackett. *Carolina Magazine* 64 (Apr. 1935): 29.

"Symbol as Need." Rev. essay of Susanne Langer's *Feeling and Form. Thought* 29 (Autumn 1954): 381–90. In *MB*, pp. 288–97.

"Truth, or Pavlov's Dogs?" Rev. of *Battle for the Mind*, by William Sargant. *America* 8 June 1957: 306–07.

"Modern Man on the Threshold." *America* 12 Aug. 1961: 612.

"Virtues and Vices in the Southern Literary Renascence." Rev. of *A Dream of Mansions*, by Norris Lloyd; *The Wandering of Desire*, by Marion Montgomery; *Judgment Day*, by Thomas Chastain. *Commonweal* 76 (11 May 1962): 181–82.

"Hughes's Solipsism Malgré Lui." Rev. of *The Fox in the Attic*, by Richard Hughes. *Sewanee Review* 72 (1964): 489–95.

"The Fire This Time." Rev. of *"I Do So Politely": A Voice from the South*, by Robert Canzoneri; *Mississippi Black Power: Three for Mississippi*, by William Bradford Hule; *Letters from Mississippi*, ed. by Elizabeth Sutherland; *Integration at Ole Miss*, by Russell H. Barrett; *Mississippi: The Long Hot Summer*, by William Mc-Cord; *Freedom Summer*, by Sally Belfrage. *New York Review of Books*, 1 July 1965: 3–5.

"The Doctor Listened." Rev. of *Children of Crisis*, by Robert Coles. *New York Times Book Review*, 25 June 1967: 7.

Rev. of *Symbolic Behavior*, by Theodore Thass-Thienemann. *Psychiatry* 33 (1970): 132–34.

"Walter M. Miller's *A Canticle for Leibowitz*: A Rediscovery." *Southern Review* 7 (1971): 572–78. Rpt. *Rediscoveries*. Ed. with an intro. by David Madden. New York: Crown, 1971. 262–69.

"The Mercy Killing." *New York Times Book Review*, 6 June 1971: 7.

Rev. of *Confessions of a White Racist*, by Larry L. King. *New York Times Book Review*, 27 June 1971: 5.

Rev. of *The Omni-Americans: New Perspectives on Black Experience and American Culture*, by Albert Murray, and *A Special Rage*, by Gilbert Moore. *Tulane Law Review* 46.5 (June 1972): 1059–70.

"The Left Hand of Sheed." Rev. of *People Will Always Be Kind*, by Wilfred Sheed. *America* 12 May 1973: 438–39.

Rev. of *Letters and Documents*, by Søren Kierkegaard. Ed. Henrik Rosenmeier. *New York Times Book Review*, 1 Apr. 1979: 1, 28–29.

"There's a Contra in My Gumbo." Rev. of *Bandits,* by Elmore Leonard. *New York Times Review,* 4 Jan. 1987: 7.

A.3. Periodicals: Articles, introductions, essays, excerpts

"The Willard Huntington Wright Murder Case." *Carolina Magazine* 64 (Jan. 1935): 4–6.

"The Movie Magazine: A Low 'Slick'." *Carolina Magazine* 64 (Mar. 1935): 4–9.

"Symbol as Hermeneutic in Existentialism." *Philosophy and Phenomenological Research* 16 (June 1956): 522–30. In MB, pp. 277–87.

"Stoicism in the South." *Commonweal* 6 July 1956: 342–44.

"The Man on the Train: Three Existential Modes." *Partisan Review* 23 (Fall 1956): 478–94. In MB, pp. 83–100.

"The Coming Crisis in Psychiatry" (Part I). *America* 5 Jan. 1957: 391–93.

"The Coming Crisis in Psychiatry" (Part II). *America* 12 Jan. 1957: 415–18.

"The American War." *Commonweal* 29 Mar. 1957: 655–57.

"Semiotic and a Theory of Knowledge." *Modern Schoolman* 34 (1957): 225–46. In MB, pp. 243–64.

"The Act of Naming." *Forum* (U. of Houston) 1 (Summer 1957): 4–9. As "The Mystery of Language" in MB, pp. 150–58.

"A Southern View." *America* 47 (20 July 1957): 428–29.

"The Southern Moderate." *Commonweal* 67 (13 December 1957): 279–82.

"Metaphor as Mistake." *Sewanee Review* 66 (Winter 1958): 79–99. In MB, pp. 64–82.

"Decline of the Western." *Commonweal* 16 May 1958: 181–83.

"Symbol, Consciousness, and Intersubjectivity." *Journal of Philosophy* 55 (17 July 1958): 631–41. In MB, pp. 265–76.

"Culture: The Antinomy of the Scientific Method." *New Scholasticism* 32 (Oct. 1958): 443–75. In *MB,* pp. 215–42.

"The Loss of the Creature." *Forum* (U. of Houston), 2 (Fall 1958): 6–14. In MB, pp. 46–63.

"Culture Critics." *Commonweal* 5 June 1959: 247–50.

"The Message in the Bottle." *Thought* 34 (1959): 405–33. In MB, pp. 119–49.

"Naming and Being." *Personalist* 41 (Spring 1960): 148–57.

"Carnival in Gentilly." *Forum* (U. of Houston), 3 (Summer 1960): 4–18. An early version of a portion of *The Moviegoer.*

"The Symbolic Structure of Interpersonal Process." *Psychiatry* 24 (Feb. 1961): 39–52. In MB, pp. 189–214.

"Red, White, and Blue-Gray." *Commonweal* 22 Dec. 1961: 337–39.

"How to Succeed in Business Without Thinking about Money." *Commonweal* 22 Feb. 1963: 557–59.

The South Today: 100 Years after Appomattox. Ed. Willie Morris. New York: Harper and Row, 1965. First appearance of "Mississippi: The Fallen Paradise," pp. 66–79.

"Mississippi: The Fallen Paradise." *Harper's,* Apr. 1965: 166–72.

"The Failure and the Hope." *Katallagete* (Journal of the Committee of Southern Churchmen), 1 (Winter 1965): 16–21.

"The Last Gentleman: Two Excerpts from the Forthcoming Novel." *Harper's,* May 1966: 54–56, 59–61.

"From Facts to Fiction." *Wash. Post Book Week,* 25 Dec. 1966: 6, 9. Rpt. *The Writer,* Oct. 1967: 27–28.

"Eleven in Opposition . . . Walker Percy: from *The Last Gentleman." The World of Black Humor.* Ed. Douglas M. Davis. New York: E.P. Dutton, 1967: 229–45.

"Notes for a Novel about the End of the World." *Katallagete,* Winter 1967–68: 7–14. In MB, pp. 101–18.

"New Orleans, Mon Amour." *Harper's,* 237 (Sept. 1968): 80–82, 86, 88, 90.

"Eudora Welty in Jackson." *Shenandoah* 20 (Spring 1969): 37–38.

"Notes for a Novel about the End of the World." *Katallagete* 3 (1970): 5–12. In MB, pp. 101–18.

"The Discussion Continues." *Commonweal* 92.18 (4 Sept. 1970): 431. Letter to editor in response to Daniel Berrigan's last published letter from the underground, "How to Make a Difference," in 7 Aug. 1970 *Commonweal.*

"Authors that Bloom in the Spring." *Publishers Weekly,* 22 Mar. 1971: 23–24.

Toward a Triadic Theory of Meaning." *Psychiatry* 35 (Feb. 1972): 1–19. In MB, pp. 159-88.

"Introduction." *Lanterns on the Levee: Recollections of a Planter's Son,* by William Alexander Percy. Baton Rouge: Louisiana State University Press, 1973. Pp. vii–xviii. Rpt. of the 1941 edition. Rpt. *A Modern Southern Reader,* ed. Ben Forkner and Patrick Samway, S.J. Atlanta: Peachtree, 1986, pp. 606–13.

"Introduction." *Sewanee,* by William Alexander Percy. New York: Frederic C. Beil, 1982. Rpt. excerpt from *Lanterns on the Levee: Recollections of a Planter's Son.* Baton Rouge: LSU Press, 1973.

" 'Uncle Will' and His South." *Saturday Review,* 6 Nov. 1973: 22–25.

"The Delta Factor." *Southern Review,* ns 11 (Jan. 1975): 29–64. In MB, pp. 3–45.

"Bourbon." *Esquire,* Dec. 1975: 148–49.

Mom, the Flag, and Apple Pie: Great American Writers on Great American Things. Garden City, New York: Doubleday, 1976. Pp. 131–35. First book appearance of "Bourbon."

"The State of the Novel: Dying Art or New Science?" *Michigan Quarterly Review* 16 (1977): 359–73.

"Questions They Never Asked Me So He Asked Them Himself." *Esquire* 88 (December 1977): 170, 172, 184, 186, 188, 190, 193–94. Rpt. Lord John Press, 1979; also rpt. *Conversations with Walker Percy,* ed. Lewis A. Lawson and Victor A. Kramer, pp. 158–81; also rpt. *A Modern Southern Reader,* ed. Ben Forkner and Patrick Samway, S.J. Atlanta: Peachtree, 1986, pp. 702–20.

"Random Thoughts on Southern Literature, Southern Politics, and the American Future." *Georgia Review* 32 (1978): 499–511. Rpt. *Harper's,* 258 (January 1979): 79–82, as "Southern Comfort: Thoughts on Southern Literature, Southern Politics, and The American Experience."

"Foreword." *A Confederacy of Dunces,* by John Kennedy Toole. Baton Rouge and London: Louisiana State UP, 1980. Pp. v–vii.

"Sunday Under Par." Excerpt from *The Second Coming. Harper's* 260 (Apr. 1980): 37–40+.

"Why I Live Where I Live." Esquire 93 (April 1980): 35–37. Rpt. *Times-Picayune* (N.O.), 4 May 1980: *Dixie Roto,* 50–53.

"A View of Abortion, with Something to Offend Everybody." *New York Times,* 8 June 1981: A–15.

"Foreword." *St. Tammany Parish: L'Autre Côté du Lac.* Gretna, LA: Pelican Publishing Co., 1981. Pp. ix–xi.

"The State of the Novel: Dying Art or New Science?" *The Writer's Craft.* Ed. Robert A. Martin. Ann Arbor: U. of Michigan Press, 1982. Pp. 206–20.

"The Orbiting Self: Reentry Problems of the Transcending Self." *Georgia Review* 37 (1983): 249–62.

"The Promiscuous Self." Excerpt from *Lost in the Cosmos. Vanity Fair,* May 1983: 49–52.

"Lost in the Cosmos." Excerpt from *Lost in the Cosmos. Omni* 5.10 (July 1983): 93–96.

"Herman Melville." *New Criterion* 2.3 (November 1983): 39–42.

"Uncle Will's House (Greenville, Mississippi Memories)." Editorial. *Architectural Digest,* 41 (1984): 44, 50, 54.

"William Alexander Percy and The Fugitives: An Exchange of Letters, with an Introduction by Walker Percy." Ed. by Jo Gulledge. *Southern Review* 21.2 (1985): 415–27.

"On the State of the Church." *National Catholic Register.* "Dialogue: Column." 62.1 (5 January 1986): 1, 7, 9.

"On Abortion, Faith, and Nuclear War." *National Catholic Register.* "Dialogue: Column." 62.2 (12 January 1986): 1, 7, 9.

"The Diagnostic Novel: On the Uses of Modern Fiction." *Harper's* 272 (June 1986): 39–45.

"Symposium on Roman Catholicism and 'American Exceptionalism'." *New Oxford Review* 54.2 (March 1987): 4–5. Issue also includes letter by Percy on p. 2: "It Takes One to Know One?"

"The Thanatos Syndrome." Excerpt from *The Thanatos Syndrome.* *Southern Magazine* 1.7 (April 1987): 58–62, 82–89.

A.4. Interviews, speeches, panels

"Seven Laymen Discuss Morality." *America,* 1 Oct. 1960: 12–13.

The Moral Curve. New York: The America Press, 1961. 11–12.

"Address of Walker Percy, Fiction Winner, National Book Awards. March 13, 1962." Distributed at the National Book Awards Meeting and available for a time from Alfred A. Knopf, Inc.

"Walker Percy: He Likes to Put Protagonist in Situation." With Harriet Doar. *Charlotte (N.C.) Observer,* 30 Sept. 1962: D-6.

"Walker Percy Talks of Many Things." With Don Lee Keith. *Delta Review* 3 (May-June 1966): 38–39.

"Work and Play." *New York Times Book Review,* 5 June 1966: 1, 60–62.

"An Interview with Walker Percy." With Ashley Brown. *Shenandoah* 18 (Spring 1967): 3–10.

"How to Get Ahead: In Fine Arts, in Writing." With Lynn Franklin. *Dixie Roto Magazine* of the *Times-Picayune* (New Orleans), 24 Sept. 1967: 11, 46–47.

"Walker Percy, the Man and the Novelist: An Interview." With Carlton Creemens. *Southern Review,* ns 4 (Spring 1968): 271–90.

"The Novels of Walker Percy." With Margaret Lee Kent. Unpublished M.A. Thesis, UNC-CH, 1969: 17, 59.

"Walker Percy: Politics, Racism, and Literature in the New South." With Louis Gallo. *Vieux Carré Courier* (New Orleans), 13 Nov. 1970: 3.

"Comments Made by Walker Percy at the Spring Authors Press Conference on March 3, 1971 in New York during National Book

Award Week." Distributed at The National Book Awards Meeting and available for a time from Farrar, Straus and Giroux. Excerpt rpt. *Publishers Weekly,* 22 Mar, 1971: 22–24.

"To Walker Percy, Man's Prognosis is Funny." With Bruce Cook. *National Observer,* 24 May 1971: 17.

"Oh, You Know Uncle Walker." With Philip D. Carter. *Wash. Post,* 17 June 1971: C–1, C–4.

"An Afternoon with Walker Percy." With Charles T. Bunting. *Notes on Mississippi Writers* 4 (Fall 1971): 43–61.

"An Interview with Walker Percy." With John Carr. *Georgia Review* 25 (1971): 317–32. Rpt. *Kite-Flying and Other Irrational Acts: Conversations with Twelve Southern Writers.* Baton Rouge: Louisiana State UP, 1972. Pp. 34–58.

"A Talk with Walker Percy." With Zoltán Abǎdi-Nagy. *Southern Literary Journal* 6 (Fall 1973): 3–19.

"The Southern Imagination: An Interview with Eudora Welty and Walker Percy." With William F. Buckley, Jr. Transcript of TV program "Firing Line." *Mississippi Quarterly* 26 (Fall 1973): 493–516.

"Walker Percy Prevails." With Barbara King. *Southern Voices* 1 (May-June 1974): 19–23.

"Walker Percy Talks about Kierkegaard: An Annotated Interview." With Bradley R. Dewey. *Journal of Religion* 54 (July 1974): 273–98.

"A Symposium on Fiction: Donald Barthleme, William Gass, Grace Paley, Walker Percy." *Shenandoah* 27 (Winter 1976): 3–31.

"Talking about Talking: An Interview with Walker Percy." With Marcus Smith. *New Orleans Review* 5.1 (1976): 13–18.

"A Talk with Walker Percy." With Herbert Mitgang. *New York Times Book Review,* 20 Feb. 1977: 1, 20–21.

"A Southern Novelist Whose CB Crackles with Kierkegaard." With William Delaney. *Washington Star,* 20 Mar. 1977: C1, C4.

"PW Interviews: Walker Percy." With John F. Baker. *Publishers Weekly* 211 (21 Mar, 1977): 6–7.

"Questions They Never Asked Me." *Esquire* 88 (Dec. 1977): 170, 172, 184, 186, 188, 190, 193–94, Rpt. Northridge, California: Lord John Press, 1979; also rpt. *Conversations with Walker Percy,* ed. Lewis A. Lawson and Victor A. Kramer, pp. 158–81; also rpt. *A Modern Southern Reader,* ed. Ben Forkner and Patrick Samway, S.J., pp. 702–20.

"Going Back to Georgia." The Ferdinand Phinizy Lecture, U. of Georgia, Athens, 1978. Rpt. *Georgia Review* 32 (1978): 499–511. Rpt. *Harper's* 258 (1979): 72–83.

"Dr. Percy on Signs and Symbols." With Henry Kisor. *Critic* 39 (1980): 2–5.

"Walker Percy Tells How to Write a Good Sentence." With Dannye Romine. *Times-Picayune/States-Item* (N.O.), 4 Sept. 1980: 4.

"The Study of Consciousness: An Interview with Walker Percy." With Linda Whitney Hobson. *Georgia Review* 35.1 (1981): 51–60.

"Interview with Walker Percy in His Home in Covington, Louisiana, January 2, 1981." With Jan Nordby Gretlund. *South Carolina Review* 13.2 (1981): 3–12.

"A Frenchman's Visit to Walker Percy." With Gilbert Schricke. *Delta* (Montpellier, France), 13 (Nov. 1981): 21–26.

"An Interview with Walker Percy." With Ben Forkner and J. Gerald Kennedy. *Delta* (Montpellier, France), 13 (Nov. 1981): 1–20.

"Symposium: I Would Like to Have Written . . ." *New York Times Book Review,* 6 Dec. 1981: 7, 68, 70.

"How to Be an American Novelist in Spite of Being Southern and Catholic." Flora Levy Lecture in the Humanities, Vol. 3, 1982, 1984. The University of Southwestern Louisiana, Lafayette.

"An Interview with Walker Percy." With Peggy Castex. Nouveaux Fragments du Puzzle Américain. Colloque du Centre de recherche de littérature et civilization nord-américaines. 24 Octobre 1981. Presses de l'Université de Paris Sorbonne (Paris IV), No. 9 (1983): 19–33.

"Walker Percy." With John Griffin Jones. *Mississippi Writers Talking,* II. Jackson: University Press of Mississippi, 1983. Pp. 3–45.

"A 'Cranky Novelist' Reflects on the Church: The 1983 Commencement Address." *The Quarterly* (Saint Joseph Seminary College, St. Benedict, La. 70457) 1.4 (Summer 1983): 1–3, 6.

"The Re-Entry Option: An Interview with Walker Percy." Editorial. With Jo Gulledge. *Southern Review* 20.1 (1984): 93–115.

"Interview with Walker Percy." With Linda Whitney Hobson. *Xavier Review* (New Orleans) 4 (1984): 1–19.

"A Conversation with Walker Percy about Thomas Merton." *Conversations with Walker Percy.* Previously unpublished interview with Victor A. Kramer and Dewey W. Kramer. Ed. Lewis A. Lawson and Victor A. Kramer. Jackson: University Press of Mississippi, 1985. Pp. 309–20.

"Percy Declines to Talk." On refusing to talk further to an interviewer from *The Paris Review* series "Writers at Work." *Times-Picayune/ States-Item* (N.O.), 7 Jan. 1985: Sect. B, p. 2.

"Famous First Words: Well Begun is Half Done." *New York Times Book Review* 90 (2 June 1985): 3+.

"Il Romanziere dell' Epoca Post-Cristiana." With Charlotte Hayes. *30 Giorni* 4.2 (Feb. 1986): 56–60.

"An Interview with Walker Percy." With Patrick H. Samway. *America* 154 (15 Feb. 1986): 121+.

"Technological Hubris." With Kim Heron. *New York Times Book Review* 92 (5 Apr. 1987): 22.

A.5. Records, Tapes, Miscellaneous

The American Literary Anthology/1. Fiction selected by John Hawkes, Walker Percy, and William Styron; Poetry selected by John Ashbury, Robert Creeley, James Dickey; Essays and Criticism selected by William Alfred, Robert Brustein, Benjamin DeMott, F.W. Dupee, Susan Sontag, and John Thompson. New York: Farrar, Straus and Giroux, 1968. Rpt. in paper by Noonday Press, 1968.

"Why Don't You Linguists Have an Explanatory Theory of Language?" Photocopy of typescript in Library of Congress. Origin of language and languages, plus bibliography. 1972.

The Southern Sensibility: Eudora Welty and Walker Percy Discuss Their Literary Tradition. Sound recording on one cassette, includes bibliography. Center for Cassette Studies, Keystone Heights, Gainesville, Florida 32656, 1974.

"Underground Solution." Satire of urban renovation in New Orleans. *Times-Picayune/States-Item* (N.O.), 6 Sept. 1984: Sect. A, p. 14.

Column on inproving education in Louisiana. *Times-Picayune/States-Item,* 23 May 1985: Sect. A, p. 25.

"From *The Moviegoer,*" pp. 466–71. "From *The Last Gentleman,*" pp. 472–75. "From *The Second Coming,*" pp. 476–86. *Mississippi Writers: Reflections of Childhood and Youth.* Vol. 1 Fiction. Ed. Dorothy Abbott. Jackson: University Press of Mississippi, 1985.

Filmscript Scenario for *The Moviegoer,* by L. M. Kit Carson [n.d.]; 180 pages; typescript reproduced from original by Filmways Inc.

B. SECONDARY SOURCES

1. Extended works
   a. books

Allen, William Rodney. *Walker Percy: A Southern Wayfarer.* Jackson and London: University Press of Mississippi, 1986.

Baker, Lewis. *The Percys of Mississippi: Politics and Literature in the New South.* Baton Rouge and London: Louisiana State University Press, 1983.

Brinkmeyer, Robert H., Jr. *Three Catholic Writers of the Modern South.* Jackson: University Press of Mississippi, 1985.

Broughton, Panthea Reid, ed. with an intro. *The Art of Walker Percy: Stratagems for Being.* Baton Rouge: Louisiana State University Press, 1979.

Coles, Robert. *Walker Percy: An American Search.* Boston: Little, Brown, 1978.

Hawkins, Peter S. *The Language of Grace: Flannery O'Connor, Walker Percy, and Iris Murdoch.* Cambridge, MA: Crowley, 1983.

Hobson, Linda Whitney. *Walker Percy.* Columbia: University of South Carolina Press, 1988.

Lawson, Lewis A., and Victor A. Kramer, eds. *Conversations with Walker Percy.* Jackson: University Press of Mississippi, 1985.

Luschei, Martin. *The Sovereign Wayfarer: Walker Percy's Diagnosis of the Malaise.* Baton Rouge: Louisiana State University Press, 1972.

Poteat, Patricia Lewis. *Walker Percy and the Old Modern Age: Reflections on Language, Argument, and the Telling of Stories.* Baton Rouge and London: Louisiana State University Press, 1985.

Taylor, L. Jerome. *In Search of Self: Life, Death, and Walker Percy.* Cambridge, MA: Cowley Publications, 1986.

_____. *Walker Percy's Heroes: A Kierkegaardian Analysis.* New York: Seabury Press, 1983.

Tharpe, Jac. *Walker Percy.* Boston: Twayne Publishers, 1983.

_____, ed. *Walker Percy: Art and Ethics.* Jackson: University Press of Mississippi, 1980. Rpt. *Southern Quarterly* 18.3 (1980).

Selected Reviews of the Above

Anderson, Thayle K. Rev. of *The Language of Grace. Literature and Belief* 3 (1983): 136+.

Bates, Randolph. "Writings about Percy: Reviews." *Southern Quarterly* 18.3 (1980): 158–63.

Borgman, Paul C. Rev. of *Walker Percy: An American Search* and *The Art of Walker Percy: Stratagems for Being. Christian Literature* 29 (1980): 91–93.

Brinkmeyer, R. H. Rev. of *Walker Percy and the Old Modern Age. Southern Literary Journal* 18.2 (1986): 132–35.

Carroll, E. T. Rev. of *Conversations with Walker Percy. Modern Fiction Studies* 32.2 (1986): 273–76.

Crane, D. Rev. of *The Language of Grace. Times Literary Supplement* 4279 (1985): 393.

Cunningham, J. Rev. of *The Language of Grace. Southern Humanities Review* 19.3 (1985): 297–99.

Daniel, P. Rev. of *The Percys of Mississippi. Virginia Magazine of History and Biography* 92 (1984): 480–81.

Desmond, J.F. Rev. of *Walker Percy. Christianity and Literature* 33 (1984): 79–81.

_____. Rev. of *Walker Percy and the Old Modern Age. Christianity and Literature* 35.1 (1985): 73–74.

Duffey, Bernard. Rev. of *The Sovereign Wayfarer. South Atlantic Quarterly* 73.2 (1974): 275.

Gaston, Paul L. Rev. of *The Sovereign Wayfarer. Georgia Review* 28.3 (1974): 540–43.

Godden, R. Rev. of *The Art of Walker Percy. Notes and Queries* 29 (1982): 277–79.

Gray, R. Rev. of *The Art of Walker Percy. Journal of American Studies* 14 (1980): 486–87.

Griffith, A. J. Rev. of *Conversations with Walker Percy. Choice* 23 (December 1985): 606.

Hendin, Josephine. Rev. of *The Sovereign Wayfarer. Modern Fiction Studies* 19.4 (1973): 603–605.

Hobson, Linda Whitney. "Generations of Percys Grew with Mississippi." Rev. of *The Percys of Mississippi. Times-Picayune* (N.O.), 1 Jan. 1984: Sect. 3, p. 8.

Holman, C. Hugh. Rev. of *The Sovereign Wayfarer. American Literature* 45.3 (1973): 476–77.

Johnson, M. Rev. of *Walker Percy and the Old Modern Age. Philosophy and Literature* 10.1 (1986): 129–30.

Kimball, Roger. Rev. of *Conversations with Walker Percy. New York Times Book Review* 4 August 1985: 9.

King, R. H. Rev. of *The Percys of Mississippi. Journal of American History* 71 (1984): 138.

Lawson, Lewis A. Rev. of *Walker Percy: An American Search. Southern Literary Journal* 12.1 (1979): 109–14.

_____. Rev. of *Walker Percy and the Old Modern Age. South Atlantic Review* 51.3 (1986): 108–11.

Lochte, Dick. Rev. of *The Percys of Mississippi. Los Angeles Times Book Review,* 1 Jan. 1984: 8.

MacKinnon, L. Rev. of *Walker Percy and the Old Modern Age. Times Literary Supplement* 4337 (1986): 536.

Mellard, J.M. Rev. of *The Language of Grace. Modern Fiction Studies* 30 (1984): 417–20.

Moore, R.S. Rev. of *The Percys of Mississippi. American Literature* 56 (1984): 438–39.

O'Brien, M. Rev. of *The Percys of Mississippi. American Historical Review* 89 (1984): 1171.

Pearson, Michael. "A Family Biography as Rich as the Percy Legacy Itself." *Atlanta Journal-Constitution,* 27 Nov. 1983: 7-G.

Rev. of *The Art of Walker Percy. Virginia Quarterly Review* 56 (1980): 47.

Rev. of *Conversations with Walker Percy. National Review* 38 (28 March 1986): 61+.

Rev. of *Conversations with Walker Percy. Publishers Weekly* 227 (24 May 1985): 66+.

Rev. of *Conversations with Walker Percy. Wilson Library Bulletin* 60 (October 1985): 71.

Rev. of *The Percys of Mississippi. Commonweal* 111 (4 May 1984): 284+.

Rev. of *Three Catholic Writers of the Modern South. Christian Century* 103 (26 Feb. 1986): 216+.

Rev. of *Walker Percy and the Old Modern Age. Christian Century* 102 (15 May 1985): 504.

Rhodes, L. Rev. of *The Language of Grace*. *Kenyon Review* 6 (1984): 129–31.

Schott, Webster. "Marriage of Two Minds." Rev. of *Walker Percy: An American Search*. *Washington Post,* 18 Feb. 1979: Sect. E, p. 50.

Sims, Barbara. Rev. of *The Art of Walker Percy*. *Notes on Mississippi Writers* 13.1 (1981): 41–42.

Spalding, Phinizy. Rev. of *The Percys of Mississippi*. *Journal of Southern History* 50 (1984): 494–96.

Stuckey, W.J. Rev. of *The Art of Walker Percy*. *Modern Fiction Studies* 26 (1981): 662–68.

_____. Rev. of *Walker Percy: An American Search*. *Modern Fiction Studies* 25 (1980): 737–40.

_____. Rev. of *Walker Percy and the Old Modern Age*. *Modern Fiction Studies* 31.4 (1986): 749–51.

Telotte, J.P. Rev. of *The Art of Walker Percy*. *Southern Humanities Review* 15 (Spring 1981): 174–75.

Thompson, J.J. Rev. of *The Language of Grace*. *Christianity and Literature* 32 (1983): 68–69.

Washburn, Delores. Rev. of *In Search of Self*. *Christianity and Literature* 36.3 (Spring 1987): 55–57.

Wood, R.C. Rev. of *Walker Percy and the Old Modern Age*. *Journal of the American Academy of Religion* 54.2 (1986): 358–59.

Yagoda, Ben. "A Lucid, Sympathetic Study of Walker Percy." Rev. of *Walker Percy: An American Search*. *Chronicle of Higher Education* 18 (5 Mar. 1979): R11.

B.1.b. bibliographies

Besterman, Theodore. *Literature: English and American, A Bibliography of Bibliographies*. Totowa, NJ: Rowman R. Littlefield, 1971.

Boyd, G.N., and L.A. Boyd. *Religion in Contemporary Fiction: Criticism from 1945 to the Present*. San Antonio, TX: Trinity University Press, 1973.

Byrd, Scott, and John F. Zeugner. "Walker Percy: A Checklist." *Bulletin of Bibliography* 30.1 (1973): 16–17, 44.

Dana, Carol. *Andrew Lytle, Walker Percy, Peter Taylor: A Reference Guide*. Ed. Victor Kramer. Boston: G.K. Hall, 1983. Pp. 59–186. For a review of *Andrew Lytle, Walker Percy, Peter Taylor,* see Elizabeth Sarcone. *Mississippi Quarterly* 37 (Spring 1984): 201–202. Primary and secondary materials.

Rubin, Louis D., Jr., ed. *A Bibliographical Guide to the Study of Southern Literature.* Baton Rouge: Louisiana State University Press, 1969.

Taylor, Desmond, and Philip E. Hagar. "The Philosophical Novel: Bibliography." *Bulletin of Bibliography* 37.3 (1980): 142–55.

"Walker Percy: A Selected Bibliography." *Delta* (Montpellier, France), 13 (Nov. 1981): 177–87.

Weixlmann, Joe, and Daniel H. Gann. "A Walker Percy Bibliography." *Southern Quarterly* 18.3 (1980): 137–57. Rpt. Tharpe, ed. *Walker Percy: Art and Ethics,* pp. 137–57.

Williams, Jerry T., ed. *Southern Literature, 1968–75: A Checklist of Scholarship.* Boston: G.K. Hall, 1978.

Wright, Stuart. *Walker Percy: A Bibliography: 1930–1984.* Westport, CT: Meckler Publishing, 1986. Primary materials.

B.1.c. dissertations and theses

Allen, William Rodney. "All the Names of Death: Allusion and the Theme of Suicide in the Novels of Walker Percy." *DAI* 43 (1982): 166A. Duke.

Alterman, Peter Steven. "A Study of Four Science-Fiction Themes and Their Function in Two Contemporary Novels." *DAI* 35 (1974): 2976–77A. U. of Denver.

Atkins, George Tyng Anselm, Jr. "Freedom, Fate, Myth, and Other Theological Issues in Some Contemporary Literature." *DAI* 32 (1971): 6529A. Emory.

Auer, Michael Joseph. "Angels and Beasts: Gnosticism in American Literature." *DAI* 37 (1976): 5117A. U. of North Carolina.

Barnwell, Marion G. "Walker Percy's American Trilogy." Thesis, Mississippi State University, 1974.

Bates, Marvin Randolph. "Walker Percy's Ironic Apology." *DAI* 39 (1978): 6755A. Tulane.

Belsches, Alan T. "The Southern Tradition: Five Studies in Memory." *DAI* 44 (June, 1984): 3682A. U. of North Carolina.

Bergen, Daniel Patrick. "In Fear of Abstraction: The Southern Response to the North in Twentieth-Century Fiction and Non-Fiction." *DAI* 31 (1970): 5389A. U. of Minnesota.

Berger, Kevin. "From Irony to Love: A Study of the Writings of Walker Percy." Thesis. San Francisco State University, 1983.

Bischoff, Joan. "With Manic Laughter: The Secular Apocalypse in American Novels of the 1960's." *DAI* 36 (1975): 2818A. Lehigh.

Borgman, Paul. "The Symbolic City and Christian Existentialism in Fiction by Flannery O'Connor, Walker Percy, and John Updike." Diss. U. of Chicago, 1973.

Bowden, Patricia Dixon Carrol. "The 'It and the Doing'; Sacramental Word and Deed in the Writings of Walker Percy." Thesis, Georgia State U., 1980.

Brinkmeyer, Robert Herman. "A Crossing of the Ways: Five Catholic Writers of the Modern South." *DAI* 41 (1980): 1592A. U. of North Carolina.

Cades, Linda J. "The Theme of Grief in Contemporary Southern American Fiction: A Study of Novels by Faulkner, Agee, Arnow, Styron, Welty, and Percy." *DAI* 44 (Apr. 1984): 3036A. U. of Maryland.

Carney, Linton. "Nathanael West and Walker Percy: The Moviegoers." Thesis, U. of North Carolina, 1975.

Cass, Michael M. "Stages on the South's Way: Walker Percy's *The Moviegoer* and *The Last Gentleman.*" *DAI* 32 (1971): 3992A. Emory.

Daley, Jamie Temple. "Modern Versions of The Pilgrim's Progress: West's *Miss Lonelyhearts,* O'Connor's *Wise Blood* and Percy's *The Moviegoer.*" *DAI* 44 (1983): 751A. U. of Notre Dame.

Dana, Carol Genevieve. "Where Tchoupitoulas Meets Annunciation: The Convergence of the American Dream and Spiritual Quest in the Novels of Walker Percy." *DAI* 42 (1982): 4826A. Georgia State.

Dale, Corinne Howell. "The Lost Cause: Myth, Symbol, and Stereotype in Southern Fiction." Diss. U. of Michigan, 1978.

Davies, Douglas D. "The Possibilities of the Hero in Three Contemporary Novels." Thesis. San Francisco State College, 1966.

Doran, Linda Kay Dyer. "Naming as Disclosure: A Study of Theme and Method in the Fiction of Walker Percy." *DAI* 37 (1976): 2179A. Peabody.

Foley, I.M. "The Theory of Language in Walker Percy's *The Message in the Bottle.*" Thesis, U. of New Orleans, 1975.

Foster, M. "Pain and Death in James Dickey's *Deliverance* and the Novels of Walker Percy." Thesis, U. of Houston, 1975.

Fox, William Henry. "Opposition to Secular Humanism in the Fiction of Flannery O'Connor and Walker Percy." *DAI* 40 (1979): 236–37A. Emory.

Freisinger, Randall Roy. " 'To Move Wild Laughter in the Throat of Death': An Anatomy of Black Humor." *DAI* 36 (1975): 6655A. U. of Missouri-Columbia.

Gallo, Louis G. "From Malaisian to Saint: A Study of Walker Percy." *DAI* 34 (1973): 7230–31A. U. of Missouri-Columbia.

Gray, Richardson K. "A Christian-Existentialist: The Vision of Walker Percy." *DAI* 39 (1978): 6761A. Ohio U.

Hall, Constance H. "Walker Percy's Women: A Study of the Women in the Novels of Walker Percy." Thesis, Stephen F. Austin State U., 1975.

Hammond, John Francis. "The Monomythic Quest: Visions of Heroism in Malamud, Bellow, Barth, and Percy." *DAI* 39 (1979): 6130A. Lehigh.

Hardie, Joseph K. " 'Mouthers and Unmakers': Theories of Language in the Work of Flann O'Brien, Walker Percy, and Charles Tomlinson." *DAI* 44 (May 1984): 3380A. U. of Oregon.

Haydel, Douglas Joseph. "From the Realistic to the Fantastic: Walker Percy's Expanding Vision." *DAI* 39 (1978): 6762A. Florida State U.

Hicks, Walker Jackson. "An Essay on Recent American Fiction." *DAI* 35 (1974): 3744. U. of North Carolina.

Hobbs, Janet H. "Alternatives to Alienation in the Novels of Walker Percy." Thesis, Virginia Polytechnic Institute, 1974.

Hobson, Linda Whitney. "Comedy and Christianity in the Novels of Walker Percy." *DAI* 43 (1982): 1545A. U. of Alabama.

Jones, Elinor B. "The Search as Pilgrimage in the Novels of Walker Percy." Thesis, U. of Georgia, 1975.

Jones, Virginia Marie. "The Grotesque as Satiric Device in Modern and Contemporary Southern Literature." *DAI* 42 (1981): 3601A. Georgia State U.

Kent, Margaret L. "The Novels of Walker Percy." Thesis, U. of North Carolina, 1969.

Killough, Barbara C. "*The Moviegoer:* The Search for an Access to Being." Thesis, U. of Houston, 1971.

Kissel, Susan Stevens. "For a 'Hostile Audience': A Study of the Fiction of Flannery O'Connor, Walker Percy, and J.F. Powers." *DAI* 36 (1975): 2824A. U. of Cincinnati.

Lacoste, Andre Pierre. "Mercy, Grace, Sin in the Religious Vision of Graham Greene, Flannery O'Connor, and Walker Percy." *DAI* 44 (1983): 166A. Tulane.

LeClair, Thomas Edmund. "Final Words: Death and Comedy in the Fiction of Donleavy, Hawkes, Barth, Vonnegut, and Percy." *DAI* 33 (1972): 5731A. Duke.

Luschei, Martin Louis. "The Sovereign Wayfarer: Walker Percy's Diagnosis of the Malaise." *DAI* 31 (1970): 5414A. U. of New Mexico.

Mack, James Robert. "Love and Marriage in Walker Percy's Novels." *DAI* 37 (1976): 4355–56A. Emory.

Madathiparampil, George J. "Prophecy in the Novels of Walker Percy." *DAI* 42 (1982): 4834A. Catholic U. of America.

————. "Theory and Themes in the Novels of Walker Percy." Thesis, Indiana State U., 1978.

Maney, Margaret Schaeffer. "The Urban Apocalypse in Contemporary American Novels." *DAI* 41 (1980): 2111A. U. of Miami (Florida).

Martin, Lovick R. "The Theme of Reconciliation and the Novels of Walker Percy." Diss, U. of North Carolina, 1972.

McGeehan, Carol Ann. "Walker Percy's *The Moviegoer:* A Detailed Study." Thesis (B.A.), Tulane, 1974.

Osinski, Barbara H. "From Malaise to Communion: A Study of Walker Percy's *The Moviegoer.*" Thesis, Lehigh, 1972.

Pearson, Michael Patrick. "The Rhetoric of Symbolic Action: Walker Percy's Way of Knowing." *DAI* 39 (1977): 875A. Pennsylvania State U.

Price, Patricia Thigpen. "The Search for Order in the Novels of Walker Percy." Thesis, Georgia Southern College, 1977.

Quinlan, P. Kieran. "Myth and Message: Paradigms of Belief in John Crowe Ransom and Walker Percy." *DAI* 45 (1984): 1400A. Vanderbilt.

Riehl, Robert Ellison. "The Ordeal of Naming: Walker Percy's Philosophy of Language and His Novels." *DAI* 36 (1975): 2812–13A. University of Texas at Austin.

Ryan, Steven Tom. "Chaotic Slumber: Picaresque and Gothic in Contemporary American Novels." *DAI* 37 (1976): 2187A. U. of Utah.

Seidman, Barbara Ann. "The Filmgoing Imagination: Filmmaking and Filmgoing as the Subjects of Modern American Literature." *DAI* 42 (1982): 4827A. U. of Illinois, Urbana-Champaign.

Seiler, Timothy Lee. "From Moviegoing to Moviemaking: Rhetorical Progression in the Walker Percy Fictive Protagonist." *DAI* 41 (1980): 255A. Indiana U.

Smith, Tyler Przekop. "Walker Percy's Fiction: The Vision of Distance." *DAI* 46.2 (1985): 426A–427A. U. of South Carolina.

Sturdivant, Mary E. "Christianity in the Novels of Walker Percy." Diss., U. of North Carolina, 1972.

Swick, Marly A. "Romantic Ministers and Phallic Knights: A Study of *A Month of Sundays, Lancelot,* and *Falconer.*" *DAI* 40 (1979): 860A. American U.

Sutton, Jane Boyce. "Kierkegaard's Idea of Possibility/Necessity in the Novels of Walker Percy." Thesis, U. of North Carolina, 1977.

Taylor, Lewis Jerome, Jr. "The Becoming of the Self in the Writings of Walker Percy: A Kierkegaardian Analysis." *DAI* 33 (1972): 1224A. Duke.

Telotte, Jay Paul. "To Talk Creatively: A Study of the Writings of Walker Percy." *DAI* 37 (1977): 6489–90A. U. of Florida.

Van Cleave, James. "Versions of Percy." Thesis, U. of North Carolina, 1969.

Ward, Carol Marie. "Movie as Metaphor in Contemporary Fiction: A Study of Walker Percy, Larry McMurtry, and John Fowles." *DAI* 42 (1982): 3996A. U. of Tennessee.

Warren, Brenda Durham. "Existential Christianity in Three Novels by Walker Percy." Thesis, Middle Tennessee State U., 1976.

Watkins, Suzanne Blackmon. "From Physician to Novelist: The Progression of Walker Percy." *DAI* 38 (1977): 6196A. New York U.

Williams, Mina Gwen. "The Sense of Place in Southern Fiction." *DAI* 34 (1973): 3440–41A. Louisiana State U.

Wineapple, Brenda. "Neo-Romanticism in Contemporary American Fiction." *DAI* 37 (1976): 5133A. U. of Wisconsin.

Wyche, Charlyne S. "A Survey of the Southern Legend in the Recent Southern Novel." Thesis, McNeese State U., 1969.

It is important to note here that three issues of the following periodicals have devoted most or all of their space to articles and interviews about Percy's fiction and non-fiction:

Southern Quarterly 18.3 (Spring 1980) entire issue; *Delta* (Montpellier, France) 13 (1981) entire issue; and *South Carolina Review* 13.2 (1981) 6 out of 8 articles. *Delta* and *South Carolina Review* timed their publications to honor Dr. Percy on his 65th birthday, May 28, 1981.

B.2.A. Periodical articles and reviews, biographical material, chapters in books. (Note: articles such as Lauder's and Taylor's articles in *Commonweal* are listed here because they are longer and more complex than many newspaper and magazine articles. The unifying characteristic of this section is that the articles are *general* but also *scholarly,* useful for research purposes.)

Allen, William Rodney. "All the Names of Death: Walker Percy and Hemingway." *Mississippi Quarterly* 36 (Winter 1982–83): 3–20.

————. "Walker Percy's Allusions to *All the King's Men.*" *Notes on Mississippi Writers* 15.1 (1983): 5–10.

Atkins, A. "Walker Percy and Wednesday Afternoons." *Humanist* 43 (July/August 1983): 33–34.

Baker, Lewis. "Planters, Gardeners, and Such." *The Percys of Mississippi: Politics and Literature in the New South.* Baton Rouge and London: Louisiana State U. Press, 1983. Pp. 174–205.

Betts, Doris. "The Christ-Haunted Psyche of the Southern Writer." *Books and Religion* 13.2 (March 1985): 1, 14–15.

Bigger, Charles P. "Logos and Epiphany: Walker Percy's Theology of Language." *Southern Review* 13.1 (January 1977): 196–206.

————. "Walker Percy and the Resonance of the World." *Southern Quarterly* 18.3 (1980): 43–54. Rpt. Tharpe, ed., pp. 43–54.

Binding, Paul. *Separate Country: A Literary Journey through the American South.* New York: Paddington Press, 1979. Pp. 33, 69–76, 147, 199, 209, 213.

Bischoff, Joan. "Walker Percy." *American Novelists Since World War II.* Ed. Jeffrey Helterman and Richard Layman. Detroit: Gale, 1978. Pp. 390–97.

Blouin, Michael T. "The Novels of Walker Percy: An Attempt at Synthesis." *Xavier University Studies* 6 (Feb. 1967): 29–42.

Boyd, G.N., and Boyd, L.A. *Religion in Contemporary Fiction: Criticism from 1945 to the Present.* San Antonio, TX: Trinity U. Press, 1973. Pp. i–99, esp. 44. Includes seven articles on Percy.

Bradbury, John M. "Absurd Insurrection: The Barth-Percy Affair." *South Atlantic Quarterly* 68 (Summer 1969): 319–29.

Bradley, Jared W. "Walker Percy and the Search for Wisdom." *Louisiana Studies* 12 (Winter 1973): 579–90.

Brinkmeyer, Robert H., Jr. "Percy's Bludgeon: Message and Narrative Strategy." *Southern Quarterly* 18.3 (1980): 80–90. Rpt. Tharpe, ed., pp. 80–90.

————. *The Catholic Writers of the Modern South: Allen Tate, Caroline Gordon Walker Percy.* Jackson: U. Press of Mississippi, 1985. 119–68.

Broberg, Jan. "Walker Percy—En udda amerikan." *Studiekamraten* 54 (1972): 119–20.

Brooks, Cleanth. "The Current State of American Literature." *Southern Review* ns 9 (Winter 1973): 273–87. Esp. 285–87.

————. "The Southernness of Walker Percy." *South Carolina Review* 13.2 (1981): 34–38.

_____. "Walker Percy and Modern Gnosticism." *Southern Review* ns 13 (1977): 677–87. Rpt. Broughton, ed., pp. 260–72.

Broughton, Panthea Reid. "Walker Percy and the Myth of the Innocent Eye." *Literary Romanticism in America.* Ed. William L. Andrews. Baton Rouge: Louisiana State U. Press, 1981. Pp. 94–108.

Buckley, William F., Jr. "The Southern Imagination: An Interview with Eudora Welty and Walker Percy." *Mississippi Quarterly* 26.4 (Fall 1973): 493–516. Rpt. transcript of television program *Firing Line: The Southern Imagination,* televised by PBS on Dec. 24, 1972. Columbia, SC: Southern Educational Communications Assn., 1972.

Byrd, Scott. "The Dreams of Walker Percy." *Red Clay Reader* 3 (1966): 70–73.

Chesnick, Eugene. "Novel's Ending and the World's End: The Fiction of Walker Percy." *Hollins Critic* 10.5 (1973): 1–11.

Coles, Robert. "On the Nature of Character: Some Preliminary Field Notes." *Daedalus* 110 (Fall 1981): 131–43. Esp. note on p. 143.

_____. "Profiles (Walker Percy): The Search." *New Yorker,* 54 (2 Oct. 1978): 43–44+. Also, 54 (9 Oct. 1978): 52–54+.

_____. "Storytellers' Ethics." *Harvard Business Review* 65 (March/April 1987): 8+.

Dabbs, James McBride. "Walker Percy." *Civil Rights in Recent Southern Fiction.* Atlanta: Southern Regional Council, 1969. Pp. 65–73.

Dollarhide, Louis. "Mississippi's Renaissance Man." *Mississippi Heroes.* Ed. Dean Faulkner Wells and Hunter Cole. Jackson: U. Press of Mississippi, 1980. Pp. 145–57.

Dougherty, David C. "Ghosts of the Old South: Walker Percy's Conservative Horrors." *West Virginia University Philological Papers* 28 (1982): 154–61.

Dowie, William, S.J. "Walker Percy: Sensualist-Thinker." *Novel* 6 (Fall 1972): 52–65.

_____. "Encountering Walker Percy." *Southeastern Magazine* (Summer 1984): 16–18.

Eubanks, Cecil L. "Walker Percy: Eschatology and the Politics of Grace." *Southern Quarterly* 18.3 (Spring 1980): 121–36. Rpt. Tharpe, ed., pp. 121–36.

Gaston, Paul L. "The Revelation of Walker Percy." *Colorado Quarterly* 20 (Spring 1972): 459–70.

Gordon, Caroline. Correspondence to Flannery O'Connor in "A Master Class: From the Correspondence of Caroline Gordon and Flannery O'Connor." Ed. by Sally Fitzgerald. *Georgia Review*

33.4 (Winter 1979): 827–46, esp. p. 830.

Gray, R. "Novels that Diagnose the Culture's Pathology." *Christianity Today* 25 (20 Nov. 1981): 78.

Gretlund, Jan Nordby. "Walker Percy: A Scandinavian View." *South Carolina Review* 13.2 (1981): 18–27.

————. "Novelists of the Third Phase of the Renaissance: Walker Percy, Madison Jones, and Barry Hannah." *Revue Française d'Etudes Americaines* 10.23 (February 1985): 13–24.

Guerard, Albert J. "Saul Bellow and the Activists: On *The Adventures of Augie March.*" *Southern Review* ns 3.3 (Summer 1967): 582–96, esp. 585.

Gulledge, Jo. "William Alexander Percy and The Fugitives, A Literary Correspondence, 1921-23." Intro. by Walker Percy. *Southern Review* 21.1 (1985): 415–27.

Hannah, A. Walker Percy, A Letter. *Horizon* 23 (1980): 72.

Hardy, John Edward. "Percy and Place: Some Beginnings and Endings." *Southern Quarterly* 18.3 (1980): 5–25. Rpt. Tharpe, ed., pp. 5–25.

Hardy, John Edward. "Percy, Walker." *Encyclopedia of World Literature in the Twentieth Century.* Vol. 4. Ed. Frederick Ungar and Lina Mainiero. New York: Ungar, 1975. Pp. 278, 281.

Helterman, Jeffrey, and Richard Layman, eds. "Walker Percy." *Dictionary of Literary Biography.* Vol. 2, *American Novelists Since World War II.* Detroit: Gale Research, 1978. Pp. 390–97. Includes selected bibliography.

Hicks, Jack. *In the Singer's Temple: Prose Fictions of Barthelme, Gaines, Brautigan, Piercy, Kesey, and Kosinski.* Chapel Hill: U. of North Carolina Press, 1981. Pp. 37, 237. Betts, R.A. Rev. of *In the Singer's Temple. College Literature* 10 (1983): 228–29.

Hobson, Linda Whitney. "Literary Landmarks: Walker Percy's New Orleans." *Diversion* 15.1A (January 1987): 38–39, 42.

————. "Man vs. Malaise, in the Eyes of Louisiana's Walker Percy." *Louisiana Life* 3.3 (July/August 1983): 54–61.

————. "Percy's South: A Nation in Microcosm." *Alabama Society for the Fine Arts Review* 3 (1981): 3–4.

————. " 'A Sign of the Apocalypse': Walker Percy." *Horizon* 23 (Aug. 1980): 56–61. Rpt. *Dialogue* 3 (October 1980) in English and in Russian.

Hoffman, Frederick J. *The Art of Southern Fiction: A Study of Some Modern Novelists.* With a preface by Harry T. Moore. Carbondale and Edwardsville, IL: Southern Illinois U. Press, 1967. Pp. 129–37.

Holley, Joe. "Walker Percy and the Novel of Ultimate Concern." *Southwest Review* 65 (1980): 225–34.

Janssens, G.A.M. "Crisis and Imagination in Walker Percy and Robert Coover." *Nineteen Eighty-Four and the Apocalyptic Imagination in America.* Ed. Rob Kroes. Amsterdam: Free University Press, 1985. 166–79.

Johnson, Mark. "The Search for Place in Walker Percy's Novels." *Southern Literary Journal* 8.1 (Fall 1975): 55–81.

Justus, James H. "William Styron, Walker Percy, James Dickey, and Reynolds Price." *American Literary Scholarship* 13 (1975): 351–53.

Kadvany, John. "Language on the Levee." *Threepenny Review* 4 (1981): 12–14.

Kazin, Alfred. *Bright Book of Life: American Novelists and Storytellers from Hemingway to Mailer.* Boston: Atlantic Monthly/ Little, Brown, 1973. Pp. 60–67.

Kemp, John R. "City of the Dead." *Southeastern Magazine* (Summer 1985).

_____. "A Novelist's View of the Novel," *Mississippi Magazine* (May-June 1985).

Kilgo, James. "Southern Literature." *The American South.* Athens, GA: The University of Georgia, Center for Continuing Education, 1979, 1981. Pp. 17–24.

Kirby, Jack Temple. *Media-Made Dixie: The South in the American Imagination.* Baton Rouge and London: Louisiana State U. Press, 1978. Pp. 160, 164–65.

Kissel, Susan S. "Walker Percy's 'Conversions'." *Southern Literary Journal* 9.2 (1977): 124–36.

Klein, Marcus. "Melted into Air." *Reporter* 36.3 (9 Feb. 1967): 61–62.

Land, Mary G. "Three Max Gottliebs: Lewis's, Dreiser's and Walker Percy's View of the Mechanist-Vitalist Controversy." *Studies in the Novel* 15 (1983): 314–31.

Lauder, Robert E. "The Catholic Novel and the 'Insider God'." *Commonweal* 101 (25 Oct. 1974): 78–81.

_____. "Walker Percy: The Existential Wayfarer's Triumph over Everydayness." *American Catholic Philosophical Association Proceedings* 56 (1982): 41–49.

Lawson, Lewis A., ed. Introduction to *Kierkegaard's Presence in Contemporary American Life: Essays from Various Disciplines.* Metuchen, NJ: Scarecrow Press, 1970. P. xvi.

————. "Kierkegaard and the Modern American Novel." *Essays in Memory of Christine Burleson*. Ed. Thomas G. Burton. Johnson City, TN: East Tennessee State U., 1969. Pp. 111–25, esp. pp. 124–25.

————. "Walker Percy." *The History of Southern Literature*. Ed. with an intro. by Louis D. Rubin, Jr., *et al.* Baton Rouge: Louisiana State UP, 1985): 505–509.

————. "Walker Percy (1916–   )." *Southern Writers: A Biographical Dictionary*. Ed. Robert Bain, Joseph M. Flora, and Louis D. Rubin, Jr. Baton Rouge and London: Louisiana State U. Press, 1979. Pp. 346–47.

————. "Walker Percy: The Physician as Novelist." *South Atlantic Bulletin* 37.2 (1972): 58–63.

————. "Walker Percy's Indirect Communications." *Texas Studies in Literature and Language* 11 (Spring 1969): 867–900.

————. "Walker Percy's Southern Stoic." *Southern Literary Journal* 3.1 (1970): 5–31.

————. "William Alexander Percy, Walker Percy, and the Apocalypse." *Modern Age* 24 (1980): 396–406. Rpt. *Another Generation: Southern Fiction Since World War II*. Jackson: U. Press of Mississippi, 1984. Pp. 122–43.

LeClair, Thomas. "Death and Black Humor." *Critique: Studies in Modern Fiction* 17.1 (1975): 6, 21–22.

————. "The Eschatological Vision of Walker Percy." *Renascence* 26 (Spring 1974): 115–22.

Leenhouts, Anneke. "Letting Go of the Old South: An Introduction to Walker Percy." *Dutch Quarterly Review of Anglo-American Letters* 15.1 (1985): 36–51.

Lehan, Richard. *A Dangerous Crossing: French Literary Existentialism and the Modern American Novel*. With a preface by Harry T. Moore. Carbondale and Edwardsville, IL: Southern Illinois U. Press, 1973. Pp. 133–45.

————. "The Way Back: Redemption in the Novels of Walker Percy." *Southern Review* ns 4 (Spring 1968): 306–19.

Lewicki, Z. "Images of the Apocalypse: George Orwell, Tadeusz Konwicki, Walker Percy." *Nineteen Eighty-Four and The Apocalyptic Imagination in America*. Ed. Rob Kroes. Amsterdam: Free University Press, 1985. 180–88.

Luker, Ralph E. "To Be Southern/To Be Catholic: An Interpretation of the Thought of Five American Writers." *Southern Studies* 22.2 (Summer 1983): 168–76.

MacMillan, Duane J., ed. *The Stoic Strain in American Literature: Essays in Honor of Marston LaFrance.* U. of Toronto Press, 1979. Pp. 179–97, esp. 180–91.

————. "Walker Percy in Canada: A Case for the Saskatchewan Sleeping Bag." *Notes on Mississippi Writers* 16.1 and 2 (1984): 3–12.

Madden, David, ed. *Rediscoveries.* New York: Crown, 1971. Includes "Walker Percy on Warren M. Miller, Jr.'s *A Canticle for Leibowitz.*" Pp. 262–69.

Maxwell, Robert. "Walker Percy's Fancy." *Minnesota Review* 7 (1967): 231–37.

May, John R. "Louisiana Writers in Film." *Southern Quarterly* 23 (1984): 18–31.

McFague, Sallie. "The Parabolic in Faulkner, O'Connor, and Percy." *Notre Dame English Journal* 15 (Spring 1983): 49–66.

Morey-Gaines, A.J. "Religion and Sexuality in Walker Percy, William Gass, and John Updike: Metaphors of Embodiment in the Androcentric Imagination." *Journal of the American Academy of Religion* 51 (1983): 595–609.

Morrow, Mark. *Images of the Southern Writer,* foreword by Erskine Caldwell. Athens: U. of Georgia Press, 1985. 60–61.

Murray, Albert. *South to a Very Old Place.* New York: McGraw-Hill, 1971. Pp. 197–209.

Newcombe, Jack. "About Walker Percy." *Book-of-the-Month Club News,* Mar. 1977. p. 4.

O'Dea, Richard J. "Percy Novels: Good News." *National Catholic Reporter,* 6 Mar. 1981: 16, 18.

Pearson, Michael. "Art as Symbolic Action: Walker Percy's Aesthetic." *Southern Quarterly* 18.3 (1980): 55–64. Rpt. Tharpe, ed., pp. 55–64.

"Percy, Walker." *Current Biography* 37 (Sept. 1976): 14–17.

"Percy, Walker." *World Authors, 1950–1970.* Ed. John Wakeman. New York: Wilson, 1975. Pp. 1126–28.

Prunty, Wyatt. "Querns, Queries, and Quahogs: Walker Percy's Reviewers on Review." Rev. and bibliography. *Georgia Review* 35 (1981): 160–66.

Rhein, Phillip H. "Camus and Percy: An Acknowledged Influence." *Albert Camus 1980.* Ed. Raymond Gay-Crosier. Second International Conference, Feb. 21–23, 1980, U. of Florida, Gainesville. Gainesville: U. Press of Florida. Pp. 257–64.

————. Some Comments on the Meaning of Twentieth-Century Art

and Literature. *Albert Camus 1980.* Pp. 32–42.

———. "Walker Percy's European Connection." *French-American Review* 7 (1983): 19–33.

Rubin, Louis D., Jr. "The Boll Weevil, the Iron Horse, and The End of the Line: Thoughts on the South." *A Gallery of Southerners.* Baton Rouge and London: Louisiana State U. Press, 1982. Pp. 197–222. Chiefly discusses *The Last Gentleman* but also Percy's ideas in general.

———, ed. *The Comic Imagination in American Literature.* New Brunswick, NJ: Rutgers U. Press, 1963. Pp. 339–48.

———, et al. "Deep Delta." *Mississippi Writers in Context: Transcripts of "A Climate for Genius," A Television Series.* Ed. Robert L. Phillips, Jr. Jackson, MS: Mississippi Library Commission, 1976. Pp. 17–33, esp. 21–22, 25–27.

———. "The South's Writers: A Literature of Time and Change." *Southern World* 1.2 (1979): 26–27.

———, et al. "Twentieth-Century Southern Literature." *Southern Literary Study: Problems and Possibilities.* Ed. Louis D. Rubin, Jr., and C. Hugh Holman. Chapel Hill: U. of North Carolina Press, 1975. Pp. 133–64, esp. pp. 138–41.

Rutschky, M. "The Saint in the Character of William Holden: The Novels of Walker Percy." *Merkur: Deutsche Zeitschrift für Europäisches Denken* 37 (1983): 576–82.

Simpson, Lewis P. "Home by Way of California: The Southerner as the Last European." *Southern Literature in Transition: Heritage and Promise.* Ed. with preface by Philip Castille and William Osborne; with intro. by C. Hugh Holman. Memphis: Memphis State U. Press, 1983. Pp. 55–70. Chiefly on *Lancelot,* but also Percy's ideas in general.

———. "The Southern Aesthetic of Memory." *Tulane Studies in English* 23 (1978): 207–27, esp. pp. 221–26.

———. "Southern Fiction." *Harvard Guide to Contemporary American Writing.* Ed. Daniel Hoffman. Cambridge, MA, and London: Belknap Press of Harvard U. Press, 1979. Pp. 153–90, esp. 180–83.

Spivey, Ted R. *The Journey Beyond Tragedy: A Study of Myth and Modern Fiction.* Gainesville, FL: U. Presses of Florida, 1980. Pp. ix–x, 139, 148–51, 153–59, 162–64. Rpt. his "Walker Percy and the Archetypes." Pp. 148–64.

———. "Religion and the Reintegration of Man in Flannery O'Connor and Walker Percy." *The Poetry of Community: Essays on the*

Southern Sensibility of History and Literature. Ed. Lewis P. Simpson. Atlanta: Georgia State U. School of Arts and Sciences. Pp. 67–79.

————. "Walker Percy and the Archetypes." *The Art of Walker Percy: Stratagems for Being.* Ed. Panthea Reid Broughton. Baton Rouge and London: Louisiana State U. Press, 1979. Pp. 273–93.

Stelzmann, Rainulf A. "Adam in Extremis: Die Romane Walker Percys." *Stimmen der Zeit* 191 (1973): 206–10.

————. "Das Schwert Christi: Zwei Versuche Walker Percys." *Stimmen der Zeit* 195 (1977): 641–43.

Stevenson, John W. "Walker Percy: The Novelist as Poet." *Southern Review* 17.1 (1981): 164–74.

Stuckey, W.J. "Percy, Walker." *Contemporary Novelists.* 2nd ed. Ed. James Vinson. New York: St. Martin's Press, 1976. Pp. 978–79.

————. "Walker Percy." *Twentieth Century American Literature.* Ed. James Vinson. New York: St. Martin's Press, 1980. Pp. 448–49.

Sullivan, Walter. *A Requiem for the Renascence: The State of Fiction in the Modern South.* Athens: U. of Georgia Press, 1976. Pp. 64–69, 72–73.

————. "Southern Novelists and the Civil War." *Death by Melancholy: Essays on Modern Southern Fiction.* Baton Rouge: Louisiana State U. Press, 1976. Pp. 66–67.

————. *Walker Percy.* Jackson: Mississippi Library Commission, 1977.

Tanner, Tony. *City of Words: American Fiction, 1950–1970.* New York: Harper and Row, 1971. Pp. 260–62.

Taylor, Lewis J., Jr. "Walker Percy and the Self." *Commonweal* 100 (10 May 1974): 233–36.

————. "Walker Percy's Knights of the Hidden Inwardness." *Anglican Theological Review* 56 (1974): 125–51.

Telotte, J.P. "A Symbolic Structure for Walker Percy's Fiction." *Modern Fiction Studies* 26 (1980): 227–40.

————. "Walker Percy: A Pragmatic Approach." *Southern Studies* 18 (1979): 217–30.

————. "Walker Percy's Language of Creation." *Southern Quarterly* 16 (1978): 105–16.

Tharpe, Jac. "Walker Percy." *Southern Quarterly* 18.3 (1980): 1–4.

Tolson, Jay. "The Education of Walker Percy." *Wilson Quarterly* 8.2 (Spring 1984): 156–66.

"Walker Percy." *Contemporary Literary Criticism.* Vol. 2. Ed. Carolyn Riley and Barbara Harte. Detroit: Gale Research, 1974. Pp. 332–35.

"Walker Percy." *Contemporary Literary Criticism.* Vol. 3. Ed. Carolyn Riley. Detroit: Gale Research, 1975. Pp. 378–81.

"Walker Percy." *Contemporary Literary Criticism.* Vol. 6. Ed. Carolyn Riley and Phyllis Carmel Mendelson. Detroit: Gale Research, 1976. Pp. 399–401.

"Walker Percy." *Contemporary Literary Criticism.* Vol. 8. Ed. Dedria Bryfonski and Phyllis Carmel Mendelson. Detroit: Gale Research, 1978. Pp. 438–46.

"Walker Percy." *Contemporary Literary Criticism.* Vol. 14. Ed. Dedria Bryfonski and Laurie Lanzen Harris. Detroit: Gale Research, 1980. Pp. 411–19.

"Walker Percy." *Critical Survey of Long Fiction.* Vol. 5. Ed. Frank N. Magill. Englewood Cliffs, NJ: Salem Press, 1983. Pp. 2087–2100.

Whittington, M.J. "From the Delta." *Delta Review* 5 (Feb. 1968): 30.

Winslow, William. "Modernity and the Novel: Twain, Faulkner, and Percy." *Gypsy Scholar: Graduate Forum for Literary Criticism* 8 (1981): 19–40.

Wolfe, Peter. "Knowing the Noumenon." *Prairie Schooner* 42.2 (Summer 1968): 181–85.

Wood, R.C. "Walker Percy as Satirist: Christian and Humanist Still in Conflict." *Christian Century* 97 (19 Nov. 1980): 1122–27.

Yardley, Jonathan. "The New Old Southern Novel." *Partisan Review* 40 (Spring 1973): 286–93.

Young, Thomas Daniel. "A New Breed: Walker Percy's Critics' Attempts to Place Him." *Mississippi Quarterly* 33 (1980): 489–98.

Zeugner, John F. "Walker Percy and Gabriel Marcel: The Castaway and the Wayfarer." *Mississippi Quarterly* 28 (Winter 1974–75): 21–53.

B.2.b. specific articles and journal reviews of Percy's work

The Moviegoer

Atkins, Anselm. "Walker Percy and Post-Christian Search." *Centennial Review* 12 (Winter 1968): 73–95.

Britton, Anne. Rev. of *The Moviegoer. Books and Bookmen* 11 (March 1966): 79.

Bryant, Jerry H. *The Open Decision: The Contemporary American Novel and Its Intellectual Background.* New York: Free Press, 1971. Pp. 273–77.

Bukoski, Anthony. "The Lady and Her Business of Love in Selected Southern Fiction." *Studies in the Humanities* 5.1 (January 1976): 14–18.

Byrd, Scott. "Mysteries and Movies: Walker Percy's College Articles and *The Moviegoer.*" *Mississippi Quarterly* 25 (Spring 1972): 165–81.

Cheney, Brainerd. "To Restore a Fragmented Image." *Sewanee Review* 69 (1961): 691–700.

Coles, Robert. "Shadowing Binx." *Literature and Medicine* 4 (1985): 151–60.

Cook, Bruce A. Rev. of *The Moviegoer. Critic* 20 (Sept. 1961): 44.

Cummings, Robert J. Rev. of *The Moviegoer. Best Sellers* 21 (15 June 1961): 122.

Filippidis, Barbara. "Vision and the Journey to Selfhood in Walker Percy's *The Moviegoer.*" *Renascence* 33.1 (Autumn 1980): 10–23.

Freshney, Pamela. "*The Moviegoer* and *Lancelot:* The Movies as Literary Symbol." *Southern Review* 18.4 (Fall 1982): 718–27.

Henisey, Sarah. "Intersubjectivity in Symbolization." *Renascence* 20 (Summer 1968): 208–14.

Hobbs, Janet. "Binx Bolling and the Stages on Life's Way." *The Art of Walker Percy: Stratagems for Being.* Ed. Panthea Reid Broughton. Baton Rouge and London: Louisiana State U. Press, 1979. Pp. 37–49.

Hoggard, James. "Death of the Vicarious." *Southwest Review* 49 (1964): 366–74.

Hyman, S.E. "Moviegoing and Other Intimacies." *Standards: A Chronicle of Books for Our Time.* New York: Horizon, 1966. Pp. 63–67.

Kostelanetz, Richard. "The New American Fiction." *The New American Arts.* Ed. Richard Kostelanetz. New York: Horizon Press, 1965. Pp. 194–236, esp. pp. 224–25.

Lawry, Edward G. "Literature as Philosophy." *Monist* 63 (Oct. 1980): 547–57.

Lawson, A. " 'English Romanticism . . . and 1930 Science' in *The Moviegoer.*" *Rocky Mountain Review of Language and Literature* 38.1–2 (1984): 70–84.

Lawson, Lewis A. "The Allegory of the Cave and *The Moviegoer.*" *South Carolina Review* 13.2 (1981): 13–18.

————. *"The Moviegoer* and the Stoic Heritage." *The Stoic Strain in American Literature: Essays in Honour of Marston LaFrance.* Ed. Duane J. MacMillan. Toronto: U. of Toronto Press, 1979. Pp. 179–97.

————. "Moviegoing in *The Moviegoer.*" *Southern Quarterly* 18.3 (1980): 26–42. Rpt. Tharpe, ed., pp. 26–42.

————. "Time and Eternity in *The Moviegoer.*" *Southern Humanities Review* 16 (1982): 129–41.

————. "Walker Percy's Indirect Communications." *Texas Studies in Language and Literature* 11 (Spring 1969): 867–900.

————. "Walker Percy's Southern Stoic." *Southern Literary Journal* 3 (Fall 1970): 5–31.

————. "Walker Percy's *The Moviegoer:* The Cinema as Cave." *Southern Studies* 19.4 (1980): 331–54.

Lehan, Richard. "The Way Back: Redemption in the Novels of Walker Percy." *Southern Review* 4 (Spring 1968): 306–19.

Lisher, Tracy Kenyon. "Walker Percy's Kierkegaard: A Reading of *The Moviegoer.*" *The Cresset* 41.10 (1978): 10–12.

Luschei, Martin. *"The Moviegoer* as Dissolve." In Broughton, ed., pp. 24–36.

"The Moviegoer." Masterplots 1962 Annual. Ed. Frank N. Magill. New York: Salem Press, 1962. Pp. 212–15.

Murphy, Christina. " 'Exalted in This Romantic Place': Narrative Voice and the Structure of Walker Percy's *The Moviegoer.*" *Publications of the Mississippi Philological Association* (1984): 55–68.

Pindell, Richard. "Basking in the Eye of the Storm: The Esthetics of Loss in Walker Percy's *The Moviegoer.*" *Boundary* 2 (1975): 219–30.

Presley, Delma E. "Walker Percy's 'Larroes'." *Notes on Contemporary Literature.* 3.1 (1973): 5–6.

Quagliano, Anthony. "Existential Modes in *The Moviegoer.*" *Research Studies* (Wash. State U.), 45 (1977): 214–23.

Regan, Robert. "The Return of *The Moviegoer:* Toole's *A Confederacy of Dunces.*" *Delta* (Montpellier, France), 13 (Nov. 1981): 169–76.

Richard, Claude. "L'Exil de Binx Bolling." *Delta* (Montpellier, France), 13 (Nov. 1981): 27–54.

Sheperd, Allen. "Percy's *The Moviegoer* and Warren's *All the King's Men.*" *Notes on Mississippi Writers* 4 (Spring 1971): 2–14.

Sims, Barbara B. "Jaybirds as Portents of Hell in Percy and Faulkner." *Notes on Mississippi Writers* 9 (1976): 24–27.

Sloan, Jacob. "Walker Percy: *The Moviegoer.*" *Existentialism in American Literature.* Ed. Ruby Chatterji. Atlantic Highlands, NJ: Humanities, 1983. Pp. 147–57.

Sullivan, Walter. "Southerners in the City: Flannery O'Connor and Walker Percy." *The Comic Imagination in American Literature.* Ed. Louis D. Rubin, Jr. New Brunswick, NJ: Rutgers U. Press, 1973. Pp. 339–48.

Tanner, Tony. "Afterword: Wonder and Alienation—*The Mystic* and *The Moviegoer.*" *The Reign of Wonder: Naivety and Reality in American Literature.* Cambridge, England: Cambridge U. Press, 1965. Pp. 349–56.

Thale, Jerome. "Alienation on the American Plan." *Forum* (U. of Houston), 6 (Summer 1968): 36–40.

Thale, Mary. "The Moviegoer of the 1950's." *Twentieth Century Literature* 14 (July 1968): 84–89.

Van Cleave, Jim. "Versions of Percy." *Southern Review* ns 6 (Autumn 1970): 990–1010.

Vanderwerken, David L. "The Americanness of *The Moviegoer.*" *Notes on Mississippi Writers* 12 (1979): 40–53.

Vauthier, Simone. "Narrative Triangle and Triple Alliance: A Look at *The Moviegoer.*" *Les Américanistes: New French Criticism on Modern American Fiction.* Ed. Ira D. and Christiane Johnson. Port Washington, NY: Kennikat, 1978. Pp. 71–93.

————. "Le Temps et la Mort dans *The Moviegoer.*" *Recherches Anglaises et Américaines (RANAM),* 4 (1971): 98–115.

————. "Title as Microtext: The Example of *The Moviegoer.*" *Journal of Narrative Technique* 5 (1975): 219–29.

Walter, James. "Spinning and Spieling: A Trick and a Kick in Walker Percy's *The Moviegoer.*" *Southern Review* 16.3 (1980) 574–90.

Webb, Max. "Binx Bolling's New Orleans: Moviegoing, Southern Writing and Father Abraham." In Broughton, ed., pp. 1–23.

Weinberg, Helen. *The New Novel in America: The Kafkan Mode in Contemporary Fiction.* Ithaca, NY, and London: Cornell U. Press, 1970. Pp. x, xii, 182–83.

Young, T.D. "Intimations of Mortality: Walker Percy's *The Moviegoer.*" *The Past in the Present: A Thematic Study of Modern Southern Fiction.* Baton Rouge: Louisiana State U. Press, 1981. Pp. 137–66.

Zamora, L.P. "The Reader at the Movies: Semiotic Systems in

Walker Percy's *The Moviegoer* and Manuel Puig's *La Traicion de Rita Hayworth.*" *American Journal of Semiotics* 3.1 (1984): 49–67.

The Last Gentleman

Broughton, Panthea Reid. "Gentlemen and Fornicators: *The Last Gentleman* and a Bisected Reality." In Broughton, ed., pp. 96–114.

Cheney, Brainerd. "Secular Society as Deadly Farce." *Sewanee Review* 75 (1967): 345–50.

Churchill, John. "Walker Percy, Wittgenstein's *Tractatus,* and the Lost Self." *Soundings: An Interdisciplinary Journal* 67.3 (Fall 1984): 267–82.

Dickey, James. "The Revolving Bookstand . . . Recommended Summer Reading." *American Scholar* 37.3 (1968): 524.

Dollen, Charles. Rev. of *The Last Gentleman. Best Sellers* 26 (1 July 1966): 133.

Donadio, Stephen. "America, America." *Partisan Review* 33.3 (Summer 1966): 448–52, esp. 451–52.

Douglas, Ellen. *Walker Percy's The Last Gentleman: Introduction and Commentary.* "Religious Dimensions in Literature," No. 11. New York: The Seabury Press, 1969.

Hall, Constance. "The Ladies in *The Last Gentleman.*" *Notes on Mississippi Writers* 11.1 (1978): 26–35.

Hicks, Jack. "The Lesions of the Dead: Walker Percy's *The Last Gentleman.*" *Etudes Anglaises: Grande-Bretagne, Etats-Unis* 32 (1979): 162–70.

Knipp, Thomas. Rev. of *The Last Gentleman. Sign* 46.1 (August 1966): 59–60.

Lawson, Lewis A. "Walker Percy's Indirect Communications." *Texas Studies in Language and Literature* 11 (Spring 1969): 867–900.

_____. "Walker Percy's Southern Stoic." *Southern Literary Journal* 3 (Fall 1970): 5–31.

LeClair, Thomas. "Death and Black Humor." *Critique: Studies in Modern Fiction* 17.1 (1975): 5–40.

Lehan, Richard. "The American Novel: A Survey of 1966." *Wisconsin Studies in Contemporary Literature* 8 (Summer 1967): 437–49, esp. 439–40.

_____. "The Way Back: Redemption in the Novels of Walker Percy." *Southern Review* 4 (1968): 306–19.

MacKethan, Lucinda. *The Dream of Arcady: Place and Time in Southern Literature.* Baton Rouge: Louisiana State U. Press, 1980. Pp. 215–17.

Morgan, Berry. Rev. of *The Last Gentleman. Delta Review* 3.3 (May–June 1966): 39.

Morse, J. Mitchell. "Fiction Chronicle." *Hudson Review* 19.3 (Autumn 1966): 507–14.

Pendleton, Dennis. *"The Last Gentleman." Masterplots 1967 Annual.* Ed. Frank N. Magill. New York: Salem Press, 1967. Pp. 184–85.

Phillips, Robert. "Southern Chronicle." *North American Review* ns 3.4 (July 1966): 37–38.

Pindell, Richard. "Toward Home: Place, Language, and Death in *The Last Gentleman.*" In Broughton, ed., pp. 50–68.

Rev. of *The Last Gentleman. Choice* 3.7 (Sept. 1966): 22.

Rev. of *The Last Gentleman. Virginia Quarterly Review* 42.4 (Autumn 1966): 133, 136.

Rubin, Louis D., Jr. "The Boll Weevil, the Iron Horse, and the End of the Line: Thoughts on the South." *Virginia Quarterly Review* 55.2 (Spring 1979): 193–221. Rpt. his *A Gallery of Southerners.* Baton Rouge: Louisiana State U. Press, 1982. Pp. 197–222, esp. pp. 206–215.

Sheed, Wilfrid. "Walker Percy: *The Last Gentleman.*" *The Morning After: Selected Essays and Reviews.* New York: Farrar, Straus and Giroux, 1971. Pp. 18–21. Rpt. of "Ravening Particles of Anxiety." *Critic* 25 (October/November 1966): 92–93.

Tanner, Tony. *City of Words: American Fiction 1950–1970.* New York: Harper and Row, 1971. Pp. 260–62.

Telotte, J.P. "Butting Heads with Faulkner's Soldier." *Notes on Contemporary Literature* 9.3 (May 1979): 7–8.

Tenenbaum, Ruth Betsy. "Walker Percy's 'Consumer-Self' in *The Last Gentleman.*" *Louisiana Studies* 15 (1976): 304–309.

Trachtenberg, Stanley. "Beyond Initiation: Some Recent Novels." *Yale Review* 56.1 (Autumn 1966): 131–38, esp. 137–38.

Vauthier, Simone. "Narrative Triangulation in *The Last Gentleman.*" In Broughton, ed., pp. 69–95.

Watkins, Floyd C. *The Death of Art: Black and White in the Recent Southern Novel.* Athens: U. of Georgia Press, 1970. Pp. 28, 37–38, 47, 58–59.

Love in the Ruins

Berrigan, J.R. "An Explosion of Utopias." *Moreana* 38 (1973): 21–26.

Bradford, Melvin E. "Dr. Percy's Paradise Lost: Diagnostics in Louisiana." *Sewanee Review* 81 (1973): 839–44.

Cheney, Brainerd. "Correspondence." *Sewanee Review* 82.1 (Winter 1974): 194–96. (Response to Bradford's review in autumn issue.)

Cogell, Elizabeth Cummins. "The Middle-Landscape Myth in Science Fiction." *Science-Fiction Studies* 5.15, part 2 (July 1978): 134–42.

Coles, Robert. Rev. of *Love in The Ruins. American Scholar* 41 (Summer 1972): 480.

Cook, Bruce. "The Search for an American Catholic Novel." *American Libraries* 4 (1973): 547–49, esp. 549.

Cormier, Robert. Rev. of *Love in the Ruins. Sign* 51.2 (Sept. 1971): 48–49.

Cunningham, John. " 'The Thread in the Labyrinth': *Love in the Ruins* and One Tradition of Comedy." *South Carolina Review* 13.2 (1981): 28–34.

Cunningham, Lawrence. "Catholic Sensibility and Southern Writers." *Bulletin of the Center for the Study of Southern Culture and Religion* 2 (Summer 1978): 7–10.

Deutsch, Alfred. Rev. of *Love in the Ruins. Sisters Today* 43 (August-September 1971): 57-58.

Fielding, Gabriel. Rev. of *Love in the Ruins. Critic* 30.1 (September/ October 1971): 69–72.

Godshalk, William Leigh. "*Love in the Ruins:* Thomas More's Distorted Vision." In Broughton, ed., pp. 137–56.

————. "Walker Percy's Christian Vision." *Louisiana Studies* 13 (1974): 130–41.

Goodwin, Stephen. "After the Faulkner." *Shenandoah* 23.2 (Winter 1972): 70–77, esp. 75–77.

Horner, Anthony. Rev. of *Love in the Ruins. Books and Bookmen* 17 (November 1971): 45.

Hynes, Joseph. "Percy's Reliques." *Cross Currents* 22 (Winter 1972): 117–20, 128.

Kennedy, J. Gerald. "The Sundered Self and the Riven World: *Love in the Ruins.*" In Broughton, ed., pp. 115–36.

Kiley, John. "Something Else." *Triumph* 6 (Dec. 1971): 32–35.

Lawson, Lewis A. "Tom More: Cartesian Physician." *Delta* (Montpellier, France), 13 (Nov. 1981): 67–82.

LeClair, Thomas. "Walker Percy's Devil." *Southern Literary Journal* 10.1 (1977): 3–13. In Broughton, ed., pp. 157–68.

Morse, J. Mitchell. "Fiction Chronicle." *Hudson Review* 24 (Fall 1971): 526–40, esp. 531–33.

Note on the use of "Thomas More" as name of Percy's hero in *Love in the Ruins. Moreana* 65–66 (June 1980): 115.

Rev. of *Love in the Ruins. American Libraries* 2 (July 1971): 762.

Rev. of *Love in the Ruins. Antioch Review* 31 (Summer 1971): 283.

Rev. of *Love in the Ruins. Catholic Library World* 44.7 (Feb. 1973): 425.

Rev. of *Love in the Ruins. Choice* 8 (Oct. 1971): 1018.

Rev. of *Love in the Ruins. Virginia Quarterly Review* 47.3 (Summer 1971): R96.

Sheed, Wilfrid. "Walker Percy Redivivus." *The Good Word and Other Words.* New York: Dutton, 1978. Pp. 127–31. Rpt. of his "The Good Word: *Walker Percy Redivivus.*" *New York Times Book Review,* 4 July 1971: 2.

Sivley, Sherry. "Percy's Down Home Version of More's *Utopia.*" *Notes on Contemporary Literature* 7.4 (1977): 3–5.

Webb, Max. "*Love in the Ruins:* Percy's Metaphysical Thriller." *Delta* (Montpellier, France), 13 (Nov. 1981): 55–66.

Weber, Brom. "The Mode of 'Black Humor'." *The Comic Imagination in American Literature.* Ed. Louis D. Rubin, Jr. New Brunswick, NJ: Rutgers U. Press, 1973. Pp. 361–71.

Westendorp, T.A. "Recent Southern Fiction: Percy, Price and Dickey." *Handelingen van het XXIXe Vlaams Filologencongres Antwerpen* (16–18 April). Ed. J. Van Haver. Zellik, Belgium, 1973. Pp. 188–98.

The Message in the Bottle

Arrington, Robert L. "The Mystery of Language." *Sewanee Review* 84.4 (Fall 1976): 127–130.

Bigger, Charles P. "Logos and Epiphany: Walker Percy's Theology of Language." *Southern Review* 13 (1977): 196–206.

Borgman, Paul C. Rev. of *The Message in the Bottle. Christian Scholar's Review* 6.2–3 (1976): 272–73.

Broughton, Panthea Reid. "A Bottle Unopened, A Message Unread." *Virginia Quarterly Review* 52 (Winter 1976): 155–160.

Caspar, Leonard. Rev. of *The Message in the Bottle. Thought* 51.201 (June 1976): 211–12.

Culler, Jonathan. "Man the Symbol-Monger." *Yale Review* 65 (December 1976): 261–66.

Dent, Huntley. Rev. of *The Message in the Bottle*. *U. of Denver Quarterly* 10.4 (Winter 1976): 141–42.

Dorenkamp, John H. "Anthony Burgess and the Future of Man: *The Wanting Seed*." *U. of Dayton Review* 15 (1981): 107–11.

Gaston, Paul L. Rev. of *The Message in the Bottle*. *Journal of Modern Literature* 5.4 (Supplement) (1976): 611–13.

Kirby, Martin. "Neither Far Out Nor in Deep." *The Carleton Miscellany* 16 (Fall-Winter 1976): 209–14.

Kline, Edward A. "Words, Words, Words." *Review of Politics* 38.1 (January 1976): 139–41.

Lawson, Lewis A. "Walker Percy as Martian Visitor." *Southern Literary Journal* 8 (1976): 102–13.

Michaels, Walter. Rev. of *The Message in the Bottle*. *Georgia Review* 29.4 (Winter 1975): 972–75.

Miller, Nolan. Rev. of *The Message in the Bottle*. *Antioch Review* 34 (Spring 1976): 369.

Murray, John J. Rev. of *The Message in the Bottle*. *Best Sellers* 35 (August 1975): 126.

Neilson, Keith. *"The Message in the Bottle." Masterplots 1976 Annual*. Ed. Frank N. Magill. Englewood Cliffs, NJ: Salem Press, 1976. Pp. 221–24.

O'Donnell, Roy. Rev. of *The Message in the Bottle*. *English Journal* 65.5 (May 1976): 75.

Parker, Frank. "Walker Percy's Theory of Language: A Linguist's Assessment." *Delta* (Montpellier, France), 13 (Nov. 1981): 145–67.

Poteat, William H. "Reflections on Walker Percy's Theory of Language: Or It Is Better to Stay with Helen Keller at the Well-House in Tuscumbia, Alabama, than to Venture to Mars and Be Devoured by the Ravening Particles." In Broughton, ed., pp. 192–218.

Rev. of *The Message in the Bottle*. *Choice* 12.10 (December 1975): 1304.

Scott, Robert L. Rev. of *The Message in the Bottle*. *Communication Quarterly* 24.1 (Winter 1976): 51–52.

Telotte, J.P. "Charles Peirce and Walker Percy: From Semiotic to Narrative." *Southern Quarterly* 18.3 (1980): 65–79. In Tharpe, ed., pp. 65–79.

Thornton, Weldon. "Homo Loquens, Homo Symbolificus, Homo Sapiens: Walker Percy on Language." In Broughton, ed., pp. 169-91.

Lancelot

Barrett, Deborah J. "Discourse and Intercourse: The Conversion of the Priest in Percy's *Lancelot.*" *Critique* 23.2 (Winter 1981–82): 5–11.

Becker, Tom. Rev. of *Lancelot. New Orleans Review* 5.4 (1978): 363–64.

Blewitt, Charles G. Rev. of *Lancelot. Best Sellers* 37 (June 1977): 73.

Brinkmeyer, Bob. Rev. of *Lancelot. Southern Exposure* 5.1 (Spring 1978): 95–96.

Bugge, John. "Merlin and the Movies in Walker Percy's *Lancelot.*" *Studies in Medievalism* 2.4 (Fall 1983): 39–55.

Cashin, Edward J. "History as Mores: Walker Percy's *Lancelot.*" *Georgia Review* 31 (1977): 875–80.

Christensen, Jerome C. "*Lancelot:* Sign for the Times." *Southern Quarterly* 18.3 (1980): 107–20. In Tharpe, ed., pp. 107–20.

Ciuba, Gary M. "The Omega Factor: Apocalyptic Visions in Walker Percy's *Lancelot.*" *American Literature* 57 (1985): 98–112.

Coser, Lewis A. "Culture and Society." *Society* 14.4 (July-August 1977): 85–87.

Dale, Corinne. "*Lancelot* and the Medieval Quests of Sir Lancelot and Dante." *Southern Quarterly* 18.3 (1980): 99–106. In Tharpe, ed., pp. 99–106.

Daniel, Robert D. "Walker Percy's *Lancelot:* Secular Raving and Religious Silence." *Southern Review* 14 (1978): 186–94.

Davis, J. Madison. "Walker Percy's *Lancelot:* The Shakespearean Threads." *Shakespeare and Southern Writers: A Study in Influence.* Ed. with an intro. by Lewis P. Simpson. (Jackson: UP of Mississippi, 1985): 159–72.

Desmond, J.F. "Love, Sex and Knowledge in Walker Percy's *Lancelot:* A Metaphysical View." *Mississippi Quarterly* 39.2 (1986): 103–109.

_____. "Walker Percy and T.S. Eliot: The Lancelot Andrewes Connection." *Southern Review* 22.3 (1986): 465–77.

Dowie, William J. "*Lancelot* and the Search for Sin." In Broughton, ed., pp. 245–59.

Epstein, Seymour. Rev. of *Lancelot. Denver Quarterly* 12.4 (Winter 1978): 97–98.

Freshney, P. "*The Moviegoer* and *Lancelot:* The Movies as Literary Symbol." *Southern Review* 18.4 (Fall 1982): 718–27.

Glassman, Peter. "American Romances: Fiction Chronicle." *Hudson Review* 30.3 (Autumn 1977): 537–50.

Johnson, Mark. "*Lancelot:* Percy's Romance." *Southern Literary Journal* 15 (1983): 19–30.

Kissel, Susan S. "Voices in the Wilderness: The Prophets of O'Connor, Percy, and Powers." *Southern Quarterly* 18.3 (1980): 91–98. In Tharpe, ed., pp. 91–98.

Kreyling, Michael. "*Crime and Punishment:* The Pattern Beneath the Surface of Percy's *Lancelot.*" *Notes on Mississippi Writers* 11 (1978): 36–44.

Lawson, Lewis A. "The Fall of the House of Lamar." In Broughton, ed., pp. 219–44.

––––––––. "Gnosis and Time in *Lancelot.*" *Papers on Language and Literature* 19 (1983): 72–86.

––––––––. "The Gnostic Vision in *Lancelot.*" *Renascence* 32 (1979): 52–64.

––––––––. "Moviemaking in Percy's *Lancelot.*" *South Central Review* 3.4 (Winter 1986): 78–94.

––––––––. "Walker Percy's Silent Character." *Mississippi Quarterly* 33 (1980): 123–40.

Lischer, Tracy Kenyon. "Walker Percy's Cerberus: Love, Sexuality, and Sin." *Christianity and Literature* 30 (1981): 33–42.

Malin, Irving. Rev. of *Lancelot. Virginia Quarterly Review* 53.3 (Summer 1977): 568–71.

Milton, Edith. "Seven Recent Novels." *Yale Review* 67.2 (December 1977): 260–71, esp. 268–70.

O'Brien, William James. "Walker Percy's *Lancelot:* A Beatrician Visit to the Region of the Dead." *Southern Humanities Review* 15 (Spring 1981): 153–64.

Oliver, Bill. "A Manner of Speaking: Percy's *Lancelot.*" *Southern Literary Journal* 15 (1983): 7–18.

Rev. of *Lancelot. Choice* 14.4 (June 1977): 536.

Smith, Larry. "Catholics, Catholics Everywhere . . . A Flood of Catholic Novels." *Critic* 37.11 (1–2 Dec. 1978): 1–8, esp. 6–7.

Smith, Laurence. Rev. of *Lancelot. Critic* 35.4 (Summer 1977): 86–89.

Stelzmann, Rainulf. "Major Themes in Recent American Novels." *Thought* 55.219 (Dec. 1980): 476–86.

Sullivan, Walter. "The Insane and the Indifferent: Walker Percy and Others." *Sewanee Review* 86.1 (Jan. 1978): 153–59.

Utter, G.H. "The Individual in Technological Society: Walker Percy's Lancelot." *Journal of Popular Culture* 16 (1982): 116–27.

Vauthier, Simone. "Story, Story-Teller and Listener: Notes on *Lancelot.*" *South Carolina Review* 13.2 (1981): 39–54.

————. "Mimesis and Violence in *Lancelot.*" *Delta* (Montpellier, France), 13 (Nov. 1981): 83–102.

Wolff, Geoffrey. "The Hurricane or the Hurricane Machine." *New Times* 8.6 (18 Mar. 1977): 64–66.

The Second Coming

Andreasen, N.C. Rev. of *The Second Coming. American Journal of Psychiatry* 137 (Nov. 1980): 1477.

Belsches, Alan T. "Life Over Death: The Use of Memory in Walker Percy's *The Second Coming.*" *Southern Quarterly* 23 (Summer 1985): 37–47.

Blewitt, C.G. Rev. of *The Second Coming. Best Sellers* 40 (July 1980): 130.

Brownjohn, Alan. Rev. of *The Second Coming. Encounter* 56 (May 1981): 86–91.

Charbonnier, D. Rev. of *The Second Coming. Critique* (Paris) (Feb. 1982): 152.

Cronin, Gloria. "Redemption for the Twice Fallen: Walker Percy's *The Second Coming.*" *Literature and Belief* 1 (1981): 113–22.

Desmond, J.F. Rev. of *The Second Coming. World Literature Today* 55 (Spring 1981): 317.

Folks, Jeffrey J. "*The Second Coming:* Walker Percy's 'Notes from Underground.'" *Notes on Mississippi Writers* 17.1 (1985): 9–17.

Fowler, Doreen A. "Answers and Ambiguity in Percy's *The Second Coming.*" *Critique* 23.2 (Winter 1981–82): 13–23.

Gramm, Kent. "Everynovelness and *The Second Coming:* Walker Percy's Fiction." *Theology Today* 37 (Jan. 1981): 487–90.

Guagliardo, H.S. Rev. of *The Second Coming. Southern Review* 17.3 (Summer 1981): 614–18.

Johnson, Greg. Rev. of *The Second Coming. Ontario Review* 14 (1981): 92–102.

Jones, Eric L. "Percy's *Parousia.*" *Southern Quarterly* 23.4 (Summer 1985): 48–56.

Kennedy, J. Gerald. "The Semiotics of Memory: Suicide in *The Second Coming.*" *Delta* (Montpellier, France), 13 (Nov. 1981): 103–25.

King, Richard H. "Two Lights that Failed." *Virginia Quarterly Review* 57.2 (Spring 1981): 341–50.

Kisor, Henry. "Dr. Percy on Signs and Symbols." *Critic* 39.4 (Sept. 1980): 2–5.

Koon, William. Rev. of *The Second Coming*. *South Carolina Review* 13 (Spring 1981): 109–110.

Malin, Irving. "Expect the Unexpected." *Ontario Review* 13 (1980–81): 95–100.

Murray, James G. "Fiction in the (very) Low 80's and Early Retrospective with (Mostly) Regrets for the Future." *Critic* 39.9 (Dec. 1980): 1–8, esp. 6.

Naughton, J. Rev. of *The Second Coming*. *The Listener* (London), 105 (5 Mar. 1981): 320.

Oakes, Randy W. "W.B. Yeats and Walker Percy's *The Second Coming.*" *Notes on Contemporary Literature* 14 (Jan. 1984): 9–10.

Prunty, W. Rev. of *The Second Coming*. *Georgia Review* 35 (Spring 1981): 160–66.

Samway, Patrick. "Rahnerian Backdrop to Percy's *The Second Coming.*" *Delta* (Montpellier, France), 13 (Nov. 1981): 127–44.

Schmitz, Neil. "Three Novels." Rev. of *The Second Coming* included. *Partisan Review* 48.4 (1981): 629–33.

"The Second Coming." Magill's Literary Annual 1981. New York: Salem Press, 1981. Vol. 2: 717.

Wood, R.C. Rev. of *The Second Coming*. *Cross Currents* 30.2 (Summer 1980): 206–10.

Lost in the Cosmos

Desmond, J.F. Rev. of *Lost in the Cosmos*. *World Literature Today* 58 (1984): 275.

Jolley, Reed. Rev. of *Lost in the Cosmos*. *Christ Today* 27 (7 Oct. 1983): 82.

Kramer, Victor A. "Strange Abstractions of Lostness." *Cross Currents* (Fall 1984): 354–57.

"Lost in the Cosmos." Magill's Literary Annual 1984. New York: Salem Press, 1984. Vol. 1: 482.

Maddux, Stephen. "A Questionnaire on Walker Percy's Latest Book." *Communio* 10 (Winter 1983): 396–400.

Rev. of *Lost in the Cosmos*. *Best Sellers* (Aug. 1983): 189.

Stelzmann, Rainulf. "Die Nichtigkeit und Grösse des Selbst: Walker Percys Anthropologie." *Stimmen der Zeit* 201 (Nov. 1983): 785–88.

Welch, W.J. Rev. of *Lost in the Cosmos*. *Parabola* 8.4 (Oct. 1983): 104.

B.3. Reviews and Articles in Newspapers and Magazines

General

Ball, Millie. "Walker Percy Star of Author's Day." *Times-Picayune* (New Orleans) 1 Aug. 1976: Sect. 6, p. 18.

"Born Today: Walker Percy." *Charlotte Observer* 28 May 1982.

Casey, Constance. "Literary New Orleans. "Publishers Weekly 229 (9 May 1986): 154+.

Cohen, Joseph. "What a Friend We Have in Walker Percy," *The Jewish Times* (New Orleans, LA) 9.18 (9 September 1983), p. 10; rpt. *The American Jewish Times Outlook* (Charlotte, NC) 48.1 (October 1983), pp. 15–16; rpt. as "The Southern Jewish Voice," *The Southern Jewish Weekly* (Jacksonville, FL) 60.32 (16 September 1983), pp. 22–24; rpt. as "Walker Percy: The Southern Jewish Voice," *The Detroit Jewish News* 84.3 (16 September 1983), p. 22.

Cook, Bruce. "New Faces in Faulkner Country." *Saturday Review* 3 (4 Sept. 1976): 39–41.

Ferguson, Anne. "A Brilliantly Evocative Tale of a Hot and Haunted City." Rev. of *A Confederacy of Dunces*. *San Francisco Examiner and Chronicle* 20 July 1980: WOR–38.

Gallo, Louis. "Walker Percy Struggles with Unbelief." *New Orleans Courier* 21–27 Sept. 1973: 10–11.

"Her Only Son, the Author . . . The Dead Author." *Charlotte Observer* 25 May 1980.

"Immortal Nominations." *New York Times Book Review* 3 June 1979: 12–13, 51.

Jenks, Tom. "How Writers Live Today." *Esquire* 104 (Aug. 1985): 123+.

Kemp, John. "Artists Escape Urban Life in St. Tammany Parish." *Times-Picayune* (New Orleans) 11 Oct. 1981: Sect. 7, p. 1.

_____. "City of the Dead." *Southeastern* 2 (Summer 1985): 25–27.

_____. Judge Ellis Removes Mystery as He Describes St. Tammany's Yesterdays." *Times-Picayune* (New Orleans) 17 Jan. 1982: Sect. 3, p. 12.

_____. "Walker Percy's Cosmic Search." Account of Percy's lecture at U. of Southwestern Louisiana in Lafayette in April. *Times-Picayune* (New Orleans) 15 Aug. 1982: Sect. 3, pp. 9, 11.

Kisor, Henry. "Percy and Toole Didn't Save Book Publishing from Trouble." *Times-Picayune* (New Orleans) 4 Jan. 1981: Sect. 3, p. 5.

"Loyola to Give Honor Degrees." *Times-Picayune* (New Orleans) 14 May 1972: Sect. 1, p. 12.

"Mississippi Institute Honors Artists, Writers." *Times-Picayune/States-Item* (New Orleans) 10 June 1981: Sect. 6, p. 12.

Mullener, Elizabeth. "Greenville Nurtures Many Writers." *TP/SI* (N.O.) 26 Feb. 1981: Sect. 7, p. 4.

————. "A Look at Other Literary Luminaries." Willie Morris evaluates Percy's work. *Times-Picayune* (N.O.) 15 Mar. 1981: Sect. 3, p. 10.

"North Lee Road: Something Old and Something New in Covington." *Times-Picayune* (N.O.) 24 July 1977: Sect. 4, pp. 1–2.

"Odds and Book Ends." *Charlotte Observer* 13 Jan. 1980.

"Roots of Many Artists, Writers in Small Mississippi Delta Town." *Charlotte Observer* 4 May 1982.

Sibley, Celestine. "*Sewanee:* A Book of Warm Memories." *Atlanta Journal-Constitution* 27 Apr. 1983.

Simmons, Mabel C. "Percy to Speak at USL (U. of Southwestern Louisiana, Lafayette) Wednesday." *Times-Picayune* (N.O.) 18 Apr. 1982: Sect. 3, p. 6.

————. "The Two Percys: Will and Walker." Rev. of *Sewanee* (Frederic C. Beil, publisher), excerpt from *Lanterns on the Levee* (1941), by William Alexander Percy, with an intro. by Walker Percy. *Times-Picayune* (N.O.) 6 Feb. 1983: Sect. 3, p. 7.

Skelton, Billy. "Percy Novels Satirical Chronicle of Fallen World." *Clarion-Ledger* (Jackson, MS) 15 Mar. 1979: B–5.

Stuart, Reginald. "Pulitzer Novel's Publication is Tale in Itself." *New York Times* 15 Apr. 1981: A–14.

————. The Return of Famous Natives to Greenville, Miss." *New York Times* 4 May 1982: A–22.

Torrens, James, S.J. "Walker Percy's Bicentennial Message." *America* 133 (25 Oct. 1975): 256–58.

Williams, Scott F. "Success Came Too Late for New Orleans Writer." Story on *Confederacy of Dunces. TP/SI* (N.O.) 18 Aug. 1980: Sect. 1, p. 13.

The Moviegoer

Bradbury, Malcolm. "New Fiction." *Punch* (London) 244.6397 (17 Apr. 1963): 573–74.

"Briefly Noted." Rev. of *The Moviegoer. New Yorker* 37.23 (22 July 1961): 78–79.

Daniel, John. "Fatality and Futility." *Spectator* (London) 210.7036 (3 May 1963): 572–73.

Davis, Douglas M. "A Southerner's *The Moviegoer* and His Perplexing Prize." *National Observer* 29 Apr. 1962: 21.

Doar, Harriet. "Former UNC Student Wins Novel Award." *Charlotte Observer* (N.C.) 14 Mar. 1962: B–12.

Fleischer, Leonore. "Paperbacks: Fiction." *Publishers Weekly* 192.16 (16 Oct. 1967): 59.

Gardiner, Harold C. Rev. of *The Moviegoer*. *America* 105 (17 June 1961): 448.

Hyman, Stanley Edgar. "Moviegoing and Other Intimacies." *New Leader* 45 (30 Apr. 1962): 23–24.

Igoe, W.J. "More than one America." *Tablet* 217 (11 May 1963): 513–14.

Kazin, Alfred. "The Pilgrimage of Walker Percy." *Harper's* 242 (June 1971): 81–86.

Kennebeck, Edwin. "The Search." *Commonweal* 74 (2 June 1961): 260–63.

Knickerbocker, Paine. Rev. of *The Moviegoer*. *San Francisco Chronicle* 14 June 1961: 30.

Massie, Robert. Rev. of *The Moviegoer*. *New York Times Book Review* 28 May 1961: 30.

McCleary, William. Rev. of *The Moviegoer*. *Library Journal* 86 (15 May 1961): 1905.

Poore, Charles. "Books of the Times." *New York Times* 27 May 1961: 21.

Rev. of *The Moviegoer*. *Booklist* 57.21 (1 July 1961): 664.

Rev. of *The Moviegoer*. *Kirkus* 29.7 (1 Apr. 1961): 339.

Rev. of *The Moviegoer*. *Observer* (London) 17 Apr. 1966: 22.

Saxton, Mark. "Shadows on a Screen, More Real than Life." *Books* 37.52 (30 July 1961): 6.

"Self-Sacrifice." *Times Literary Supplement* 29 Mar. 1963: 221.

Serebnick, Judith. "First Novelists—Spring 1961." *Library Journal* 86.3 (1 Feb. 1961): 597.

"Story of a Novel: How it Won Prize." *New York Times* 15 Mar. 1962: 25.

"The Sustaining Stream." *Time* 18 (1 Feb. 1963): 82–84.

Taubman, Robert. "Feeling Better." *New Statesman* 65.1674 (12 Apr. 1963): 527.

"Two True Sounds from Dixie." *Time* 77.21 (19 May 1961): 105.

The Last Gentleman

Braybrooke, Neville. "The Cruel Time." *Spectator* (London) No. 7235 (24 Feb. 1967): 228.

Buitenhuis, Peter. "A Watcher, A Listener, a Wanderer." *New York Times Book Review* 26 June 1966: 5.

Butcher, Fanny. "Tale with a Picaresque Quality." *Chicago Tribune Books Today* 24 July 1966: 10.

Casey, Florence. "Coming in from the Cold." *Christian Science Monitor* 23 June 1966: 7.

Christopher, Michael. "*The Last Gentleman,* Authority, and Papa Hemingway." *U.S. Catholic* 32.3 (July 1966): 47–48.

Crews, Frederick C. "The Hero as 'Case'." *Commentary* 42.3 (Sept. 1966): 100–102.

Davis, Douglas M. "From Mr. Percy, a Temptation Play for Folk-Rock Age." *National Observer* 5.24 (13 June 1966): 22.

DeMott, Benjamin. "The Good and the True." *Wash. Post Book Week* 12 June 1966: 2, 9.

"Fiction: The American Game of Happy Families." *Times Literary Supplement* 21 Dec. 1967: 1233.

Fleischer, Leonore. "Paperbacks: Fiction." *Publishers Weekly* 193.5 (29 Jan. 1968): 100.

Goodman, Walter. "An Elegant Quest for Ordinariness." *Life* 60.25 (24 June 1966): 20.

Grumbach, Doris. "Book Reviews." *America* 114.25 (18 June 1966): 858.

"Guidebook for Lost Pilgrims." *Time* 87.24 (17 June 1966): 104.

Hayes, Richard. "Books: Critics' Choice for Christmas." *Commonweal* 87.9 (1 Dec. 1967): 308.

Hicks, Granville. "One of the Roaming Kind." *Saturday Review* 49 (18 June 1966): 29–30.

"In the Southern Grain." *Newsweek* 67 (10 June 1966): 106, 108.

Johnson, Lucy. "Percy and Amis." *Progressive* 30 (Oct. 1966): 49–50.

Kitching, Jessie. Rev. of *The Last Gentleman*. *Publishers Weekly* 189.19 (9 May 1966): 76.

Lee Hermione. Rev. of English reissues of *The Last Gentleman* and *Love in the Ruins*. *New Statesman* 95 (3 Mar. 1979): 294–95.

McNaspy, C.J. "Books: Critics' Choices for Christmas." *Commonweal* 85.9 (2 Dec. 1966): 268–69.

Oates, Joyce Carol. "Gentleman Without a Past." *Nation* 203.4 (8 Aug. 1966): 129–30.

Petersen, Clarence. "Paperbacks: Out of the Draft." *Wash. Post Book World* 10 Mar. 1968: 11.

Pine, John C. Rev. of *The Last Gentleman*. *Library Journal* 91.11 (1 June 1966): 2877.

Poore, Charles. "A Candide in a Brooks Brothers Shirt." *New York Times* 16 June 1966: 45.

Price, R.G.G. "New Novels." *Punch* (London) 252.6596 (8 Feb. 1967): 210.

Rev. of *The Last Gentleman*. *Booklist* 63.1 (1 Sept. 1966): 34.

Rev. of *The Last Gentleman*. *Kirkus* 34 (15 Apr. 1966): 444.

Rosenthal, Raymond. "The Ceremony of Innocence." *New Leader* 49.13 (20 June 1966): 22–23.

Sheed, Wilfrid. "Additions to the Galaxy." *National Catholic Reporter* 3 (8 Feb. 1967): 7.

Tracy, Honor. "Humidification Engineer." *New Republic* 154 (18 June 1966): 27–28.

Wain, John. "The Insulted and Injured." *New York Times Book Review* 7.1 (28 July 1966): 22–24.

Wilkie, Brian. Rev. of *The Last Gentleman*. *Commonweal* 84.19 (19 Aug. 1966): 537–39.

Love in the Ruins

Anderson, David C. "Mr. Percy's Positive Statement." *Wall Street Journal* 17 May 1971: 12.

Announcement of *Love in the Ruins* in paper, published by Avon Books. *Wash. Post Book World* 11 (1 Mar. 1981): 12.

Avant, John Alfred. Rev. of *Love in the Ruins*. *Library Journal* 96 (15 May 1971): 1728.

Broyard, Anatole. "Apocalypses and Other Ills." *New York Times* 15 May 1971: 29.

Catinella, Joseph. Rev. of *Love in the Ruins*. *Saturday Review* 54 (15 May 1971): 42–43.

Davenport, Guy. "Mr. Percy's Look at Chaos, 1983." *Life* 70 (21 May 1971): 16.

Duffy, Martha. "Lapsometer Legend." *Time* 97 (17 May 1971): 94.

East, Charlie. "Sniper Fiction Comes True." *Times-Picayune* (N.O.) 11 Jan. 1973: Sect. 1, pp. 1, 16.

Garvey, John. "Fantastic Stories." *Commonweal* 102 (1 Aug. 1975): 315.

Hill, William B., S.J. Rev. of *Love in the Ruins*. *America* 124 (22 May 1971): 548.

Janeway, Elizabeth. "The End of the World is Coming." *Atlantic* 228 (Aug. 1971): 87–90.

"Lapsed from Grace." *Times Literary Supplement* 1 Oct. 1971: 1165.

Lee, Hermione. Rev. of English reissues of *The Last Gentleman* and *Love in the Ruins*. *New Statesman* 95 (3 Mar. 1979): 294–95.

Marsh, Pamela. "Tomorrow the World Ends." *Christian Science Monitor* 3 June 1971: 10.

McPherson, William. "The Greening and the Crumbling." *Washington Post* 17 June 1971: C–1, C–6.

McGuane, Thomas. Rev. of *Love in the Ruins*. *New York Times Book Review* 23 May 1971: 7, 37.

Murray, Michele. "Bad Catholic Stars in Crazy Plot." *National Catholic Reporter* 7 (27 Aug. 1971): 7.

Pettingell, Phoebe. "Walker Percy's Sci-Fi Detour." *New Leader* 54.10 (17 May 1971): 11–12.

Prescott, Peter S. Rev. of *Love in the Ruins*. *Newsweek* 77 (17 May 1971): 106–107.

––––––––. "The Year in Books: A Personal Report." *Newsweek* 78 (27 Dec. 1971): 60.

Pritchett, V.S. "Clowns." *New York Review of Books* 16 (1 July 1971): 15.

Rev. of *Love in the Ruins*. *Booklist* 67 (1 July 1971): 895.

Rev. of *Love in the Ruins*. *Kirkus* 39 (15 Mar. 1971): 319.

Rev. of *Love in the Ruins*. *Publishers Weekly* 199 (29 Mar. 1971): 44.

Rev. of *Love in the Ruins*. *Publishers Weekly* 201 (27 Mar. 1972): 80.

Rule, Philip C. Rev. of *Love in the Ruins*. *America* 124 (12 June 1971): 617.

"1971: A Selection of Noteworthy Titles." *New York Times Book Review* 5 Dec. 1971: 83.

Sheed, Wilfrid. "The Good Word: *Walker Percy Redivivus.*" *New York Times Book Review* 4 July 1971: 2. Rpt. his *The Good Word and Other Words*. New York: E.P. Dutton, 1978. Pp. 127–31.

Simmons, Mabel C. "Turning Over a New Leaf." Announcement of *Love in the Ruins* in paper by Avon/Bard. *Times-Picayune* (N.O.) 15 Feb. 1981: Sect. 3, p. 8.

Sissman, L.E. "Inventions." *New Yorker* 11 Sept. 1971: 121–24.

Smith, Julian. "Elegant Paranoia." *Christian Century* 88 (7 July 1971): 835.

Taylor, Lewis J., Jr. "Walker Percy and the Self." *Commonweal* 100 (10 May 1974): 233–36.

Taylor, Mark. Rev. of *Love in the Ruins*. *Commonweal* 95 (29 Oct.

1971): 118-19.

Theroux, Paul. "Christian Science-Fiction." *Wash. Post Book World* 16 May 1971: 4.

VanBrunt, H.L. "The Headiest, Happiest Holiday Gifts: Books." *Saturday Review* 54 (27 Nov. 1971): 46.

Wills, Garry. "Catholic Faith and Fiction." *New York Times Book Review* 16 Jan. 1972: 1-2. Reply to Wilfrid Sheed's review, above.

Yardley, Jonathan. "Stethoscope of the Spirit." *New Republic* 164 (22 May 1971): 25-26.

The Message in the Bottle

Appleyard, J.A. "Critic's Choice for Christmas." *Commonweal* 102 (5 Dec. 1976): 597.

Boatwright, James. Rev. of *The Message in the Bottle. New Republic* 173 (19 July 1975): 28-29.

Ciardi, John. "Why Is 20th Century Man So Sad?" *Chicago Tribune Book World* 29 June 1975: 6.

Crain, Jane Larkin. Rev. of *The Message in the Bottle. Saturday Review* 2 (28 June 1975): 24.

Cuffe, Edwin D. "Chickens Have No Myths." *America* 133.4 (16 Aug. 1975): 76-77.

Fuller, Edmund. Rev. of *The Message in the Bottle. Wall Street Journal* 14 July 1975: 8.

Gray, Paul. "Yoknapatawpha Blues." *Time* 108.13 (27 Sept. 1976): 92-93.

Kenner, Hugh. "On Man the Sad Talker." *National Review* 27.35 (12 Sept. 1975): 1000-1002.

King, Richard H. Rev. of *The Message in the Bottle. New Leader* 58 (13 Oct. 1975): 18-19.

LeClair, Thomas. Rev. of *The Message in the Bottle. New York Times Book Review* 8 June 1975: 6.

McLellan, Joseph. "Paperbacks." *Washington Post Book World* 16 May 1976: 14.

McMurtry, Larry. "What Language Reveals—And What It Conceals." *Wash. Post Book World* 19 May 1975: B-6.

McNaspy, C.J. " 'Why Does Man Feel So Sad?' " *National Catholic Reporter* 11 (19 Aug. 1975): 7.

Mongelluzzo, Bill. "Novelist Bored, Turns to Essays." *Times-Picayune* (N.O.) 16 May 1975: Sect. 5, p. 7.

Nagel, Thomas. Rev. of *The Message in the Bottle*. *New York Review of Books* 23.14 (18 Sept. 1975): 54–56.

Rev. of *The Message in the Bottle*. *Booklist* 72.1 (1 Sept. 1975): 14.

Rev. of *The Message in the Bottle*. *Kirkus* 43.8 (15 April 1975): 497.

Rev. of *The Message in the Bottle*. *New York Times Book Review* 7 Dec. 1975: 70.

Rev. of *The Message in the Bottle*. *Publishers Weekly* 207 (28 April 1975): 42.

Tyler, Anne. "The Topic Is Language—With Love and Skill." *National Observer* 14 (19 July 1975): 21.

Wood, Ralph. Rev. of *The Message in the Bottle*. *Christian Century* 92 (3 Dec. 1976): 1115.

Zaidman, Bernard. Rev. of *The Message in the Bottle*. *Library Journal* 100.14 (Aug. 1975): 1417.

Lancelot

Barnes, Julian. "Pantyhose." *New Statesman* 94.2431 (21 Oct. 1977): 556–57.

Chesnick, Eugene. "De Contemptu Mundi." *Nation* 224.17 (30 April 1977): 533.

"A Christmas Potpourri of Books." *Wall Street Journal* 15 Dec. 1977: 20.

Christopher, Michael. "Days of Thorn and Roses." *U.S. Catholic* 42.8 (Aug. 1977): 49–51.

Cook, Bruce. "The Last Man in America Who Believes in Love." *Saturday Review* 4 (19 Mar. 1977): 28–29.

Cuffe, E.D. "Percy and Cheever: Prison as Prism." *America* 136 (12 Mar. 1977): 220–21.

Davis, Hope Hall. Rev. of *Lancelot*. *New Leader* 60.9 (25 Apr. 1977): 14–15.

Dubus, Andre. "Paths to Redemption." *Harper's* 254.1523 (Apr. 1977): 86–88.

Egerton, John. "Memorable Madman." *Progressive* 41 (June 1977): 40–41.

Foote, Bud. "A New Lancelot Seeks His Knighthood." *National Observer* 12 Mar. 1977: 19.

Ford, Richard. "Walker Percy: Not Just Whistling Dixie." *National Review* 29 (13 May 1977): 558, 560–64.

French, Philip. "Communing with Camus." *Times Literary Supplement* 28 Oct. 1977: 1259.

Fuller, Edmund. "A Cutting Satire on Modern Life." *Wall Street Journal* 17 Mar. 1977: 18.

Gardner, John. "Moral Fiction." *Saturday Review* 5.13 (1 Apr. 1978): 29–30, 32–33.

_____. Rev. of *Lancelot*. *New York Times Book Review* 20 Feb. 1977: 1, 16.

Gray, Paul. "Questing after an Unholy Grail." *Time* 109 (7 Mar. 1977): 86–87.

Greeley, Andrew. "Novelists of the Madhouse." *Chicago Tribune* 9 June 1977: Sect. 4, p. 4.

Griffith, Thomas. "Moral Tales for a Depraved Age." *Atlantic* 240.1 (July 1977): 20–21.

Guidry, Frederick. "Walker Percy's 'Lancelot.' " *Christian Science Monitor* 2 Mar. 1977: 23.

Iyer, Pico. "A Sad Tidiness: Walker Percy and the South." *London Magazine* 18.1 (Apr. 1978): 62–66.

Kendall, Elaine. "The Degradation of Lancelot in an Uncourtly Age." *Los Angeles Times Book Review* 13 Mar. 1977: 6.

Lardner, Susan. Rev. of *Lancelot*. *New Yorker* 53 (2 May 1977): 141–44.

Lehmann-Haupt, Christopher. "Camelot Lost." *New York Times* 17 Feb. 1977: 37.

Locke, Richard. "Novelists as Preachers." *New York Times Book Review* 17 Apr. 1977: 3, 52.

McNaspy, C.J. "Sick World Diagnosed." *National Catholic Reporter* 13 (6 May 1977): 16.

Mulligan, Hugh A. "Doctor Is In—at the Typewriter." *Los Angeles Times* 4 Dec. 1977: Sect. V, pp. 18–19.

_____. "Ills of the Human Condition Diagnosed by Novelist Percy." *Times-Picayune* (N.O.) 10 July 1977: Sect. 2, p. 4.

Oates, Joyce Carol. Rev. of *Lancelot*. *New Republic* 176.6 (5 Feb. 1977): 32–34.

Prescott, Peter S. "Unholy Knight." *Newsweek* 89 (28 Feb. 1977): 73–74.

Price, Reynolds. "God and Man in Louisiana." *Wash. Post Book World* 27 Feb. 1977: E-7, E-10.

Rev. of *Lancelot*. *Booklist* 73.12 (15 Feb. 1977): 879.

Rev. of *Lancelot*. *Christian Century* 94 (6 July 1977): 634–36.

Rev. of *Lancelot*. *Kirkus* 45.1 (1 Jan. 1977): 16.

Rev. of *Lancelot*. *New York Times Book Review* 23 April 1978: 43.

Rev. of *Lancelot*. *Publishers Weekly* 211.2 (10 Jan. 1977): 66.

Rev. of *Lancelot*. *Rolling Stone* 7 Apr. 1977: 87.

T., A. Rev. of *Lancelot*. *West Coast Review of Books* 3 (May 1977): 33.

Todd, Richard. "Lead Us into Temptation, Deliver Us Evil." *Atlantic* 239.3 (Mar. 1977): 113–15.

Towers, Robert. "Southern Discomfort." *New York Review of Books* 24 (31 Mar. 1977): 6–8.

Wiehe, P.L. Rev. of *Lancelot*. *Library Journal* 102.5 (1 Mar. 1977): 633.

Will, George. "In Literature and Politics, a Quest for Values." *Wash. Post Book World* 31 Mar. 1977: A–15.

Wood, Ralph. "Damned in the Paradise of Sex." *Christian Century* 90 (13 July 1977): 634–36.

Yount, John. "Walker Percy's Funhouse Mirror: More True than Distorted." *Chicago Tribune Book World* 27 Feb. 1977: 1.

The Second Coming

Announcement of *The Second Coming* in paper by Pocket Books. *Wash. Post Book World* 11 (16 Aug. 1981): 12.

Atchity, Kenneth John. "The Fictional Five: Of Life and Death, Eloquence and Silence." *Los Angeles Times Book Review* 9 Nov. 1980: 1.

Atlas, James. "Portrait of Mr. Percy." *New York Times Book Review* 85 (29 June 1980): 1, 30–31.

Balliett, Whitney. "Will and Allison." *New Yorker* 56 (22 Dec. 1980): 86, 88.

Barkham, John. "Love in a Moral Swamp of Confusion." *San Francisco Examiner and Chronicle* 3 Aug, 1980: WOR–38.

Batchelor, John Calvin. "The Percy Perplex." *Village Voice* 9–15 July 1980: 34.

Boles, Paul Darcy. "Author-as-God View Flaws *Second Coming*." *Atlanta Journal-Constitution* 27 July 1980: Sect. E, pp. 4–5.

Bonner, Thomas, Jr. "Percy Characters Wander in a Symbolic Wilderness." *Times-Picayune* (N.O.) 20 July 1980: Sect. 3, p. 8.

Broyard, Anatole. Rev. of *The Second Coming*. *New York Times* 3 July 1980: C–20.

"Checklist of Notable Books of 1980 Briefly Reviewed." *Los Angeles Times* 12 Jan. 1981: Sect. B, p. 6.

Clark, Lindley H., Jr. "A Christmas Potpourri of Books." *Wall Street Journal* 11 Dec. 1980: 26.

Clemons, Walter. "Lay Preacher." *Newsweek* 96 (7 July 1980): 66.

DeMott, Benjamin. "A Thinking Man's Kurt Vonnegut." *Atlantic* 246.1 (July 1980): 81–84.

Donavin, Denise P. Rev. of *The Second Coming. Booklist* 76.20 (15 June 1980): 1464–65.

Egerton, John. "Quiet Chaos." *Progressive* 44.10 (Oct. 1980): 58–59.

"Five Major U.S. Writers Selected for Honors." *Los Angeles Times* 22 Nov. 1980: Part II, p. 1.

Fremont-Smith, Eliot. "The Trickle-Down Theory of Uplift." *Village Voice* 31 Dec.–6 Jan. 1981: 32.

Fuller, Edmund. "A Conversation with Walker Percy." *Wall Street Journal* 16 July 1980: 24.

————. "Walker Percy's Profoundly Satisfying Novel." *Wall Street Journal* 23 June 1980: 22.

Gilder, Joshua. Rev. of *The Second Coming. American Spectator* 13.10 (Oct. 1980): 34–35. For follow-up, see "Tunney vs. Gilder." Lengthy exchange between Gilder and Susan Tunney over merits of Joshua Gilder's rev. "Special Correspondance." *American Spectator,* Jan. 1981.

Gilman, Richard. Rev. of *The Second Coming. New Republic* 183 (5 July 1980): 29–31.

Gray, Paul. "Blues in the New South." *Time* 116.2 (14 July 1980): 51, 54.

Guillaud, Betty. "A Sign and Time." *TP/SI* (N.O.) 18 July 1980: Sect. 4, p. 6.

Hope, N. Rev. of *The Second Coming. Spectator* 246 (14 Feb. 1981): 23–24.

Kemp, Peter. "Back to Life." *Times Literary Supplement* 4060 (23 Jan. 1981): 77-D. See also 22 Jan. 1981: 12-F.

Kendall, Elaine. "Special Love as a Guide to Renewed Hope." *Los Angeles Times* 27 July 1980: Sect. 1-R, p. 4.

Kirkeby, Marc. "Percy: He Can See Clearly Now." *Los Angeles Times Calendar* 3 Aug. 1980: 52.

Levin, Bernard. "Method in His Madness." Rev. *The Second Coming. Sunday Times* (London) 8 Feb. 1981: 43.

Lisher, Tracy Kenyon. Rev. of *The Second Coming. Christian Century* 97 (15 Oct. 1980): 979.

Lyons, Gene. "Deep Hidden Meaning." *Nation* 231 (16 Aug. 1980): 157–58.

Merkin, Daphne. "Lost Souls." *New Leader* 63 (28 July 1980): 15–16.

Muther, Elizabeth. Rev. of *The Second Coming*. *Christian Science Monitor* 20 Aug. 1980: 17.

"Newspaper Literary Prize Awarded to Walker Percy." *TP/SI* (N.O.) 27 Nov. 1980: Sect. 6, p. 20.

"Notable Books of 1980: A Checklist." *Christian Science Monitor* 12 Jan. 1981: B-6.

"The Passion in Percy's Simple Words." *Charlotte Observer* 13 July 1980.

Reedy, Gerald. Rev. of *The Second Coming*. *Commonweal* 107 (29 Aug. 1980): 471.

Rev. of *The Second Coming*. *Kirkus* 48.9 (1 May 1980): 602–603.

Rev. of *The Second Coming*. *Los Angeles Times Book Review* 27 July 1980: 4.

Rev. of *The Second Coming*. *Publishers Weekly* 217.20 (23 May 1980): 70. See also 19 June 1981: 98.

Rev. of *The Second Coming*. *San Francisco Chronicle* 29 June 1980: WOR 46.

Rev. of *The Second Coming*. *Saturday Review* 7 (Aug. 1980): 95.

Romano, John. "A Novel of Powerful Pleasures." *New York Times Book Review* 29 June 1980: 1, 28–29.

Samway, P.H. Rev. of *The Second Coming*. *America* 145 (4 July 1981): 18–19.

Sipper, Ralph B. "A Rich World but Bankrupt of Souls." *San Francisco Examiner and Chronicle*. 29 June 1980: WOR–46.

Spears, Monroe K. "Return of *The Last Gentleman*." *Wash. Post Book World* 20 July 1980: 1–B.

Tate, J.L. "Percy's Reprise." *National Review* 32.22 (31 Oct. 1980): 1338–40.

Tinniswood, Peter. "Fiction: *The Second Coming* by Walker Percy." *London Times* 22 Jan. 1981: 12.

Towers, Robert. "To the Greenhouse." *New York Review of Books* 27.13 (14 Aug. 1980): 39–41.

Walters, Ray. Announcement of *The Second Coming* published in paper by Pocket Books. *New York Times Book Review* 86 (26 July 1981): 23.

Wiehe, Janet. Rev. of *The Second Coming*. *Library Journal* 105 (July 1980): 1541–42.

Williams, Thomas. "A Walker Percy Novel Puzzles over the Farce of Existence." *Chicago Tribune Book World* 29 June 1980: Sect. 7, p. 1.

Wood, R.C. "Walker Percy as Satirist: Christian and Humanist Still in Conflict." *Christian Century* 97 (19 Nov. 1980): 1122–27.

Lost in the Cosmos

Announcement of *Lost in the Cosmos* in paper by Washington Square/ Pocket Books. *New York Times Book Review* 89 (10 June 1984): 36.

Beatty, Jack. Rev. of *Lost in the Cosmos*. *New Republic* 189 (11 July 1983): 38–39.

Brosnahan, John. Rev. of *Lost in the Cosmos*. *Booklist* 79 (15 Mar. 1983): 931.

Broyard, Anatole. Rev. of *Lost in the Cosmos*. *New York Times* 11 June 1983: 12.

Clecak, Peter. Rev. of *Lost in the Cosmos*. *Commonweal* 110 (17 June 1983): 372–73. See also Burris, Keith. Letter discussing Clecak rev. of *Lost in the Cosmos*. *Commonweal* 110 (23 Sept. 1983): 508.

Cumming, Joe. "Human Walker Percy vs. 'Cosmos' Carl Sagan." *Atlantic Journal-Constitution* 17 Apr. 1983: 11–H.

"A Deadly Game of 20 Questions." *San Francisco Chronicle* 9 Sept. 1983, Rev. Sect.

Disch, Thomas M. "Walker Percy's Summa Semiotica." *Wash. Post Book World* 19 June 1983: 5.

Eder, Richard. Rev. of *Lost in the Cosmos*. *Los Angeles Times Book Review* 5 June 1983: 1, 12.

Fuller, Edmund. "The Bookshelf: You and the Universe, in Properly Readable Form." *Wall Street Journal* 201 (31 May 1983): 28.

Gray, Francine duPlessix. Rev. of *Lost in the Cosmos*. *New York Times Book Review* 88 (5 June 1983): 9.

Hobson, Linda Whitney. "Percy's Shocking 'Last Self-Help' Text." *Times-Picayune* (N.O.): 12 June 1983: Sect. 3, p. 6.

Hutchinson, Paul E. Rev. of *Lost in the Cosmos*. *Library Journal* 108 (15 May 1983): 1004.

Kaufman, James. Rev. of *Lost in the Cosmos*. *Christian Science Monitor* 76 (6 July 1984): B–8.

Lochte, Dick. Rev. of *Lost in the Cosmos*. *Los Angeles Times Book Review* 22 May 1983: 18.

"*Los Angeles Times* 1983 Book Prize." Announcement of Percy's *Lost in the Cosmos* winning the Book Prize. *Los Angeles Times Book Review* 20 Nov. 1983: 1.

"*Lost in the Cosmos:* Walker Percy Writes to Help Us Recognize Our Malaise." *Charlotte Observer,* 5 June 1983.

Lyons, Gene. Rev. of *Lost in the Cosmos. Newsweek* 101 (13 June 1983): 72–B.

Miles, Jack. "Nominees, 1983 Current Interest Prize." Various writers discuss their putative favorites. Percy's is William Least Heat Moon's *Blue Highways. Los Angeles Times Book Review* 16 Oct. 1983: 4.

Morrow, Mark. Rev. of *Lost in the Cosmos. Los Angeles Times* 10 Aug. 1983: View, Part V, pp. 1, 4.

Nachman, Gerald. "Early Warning Signs." *San Francisco Chronicle* 12 Jan. 1982.

"Percy's Next Message Is More than a Mouthful." *Charlotte Observer* 2 Jan. 1983.

Rev. of *Lost in the Cosmos. America* 154 (15 Feb. 1986): 1.

Rev. of *Lost in the Cosmos. New Yorker* 59 (18 July 1983): 97.

Rev. of *Lost in the Cosmos. Progressive* 47 (Oct. 1983): 42–43.

Rev. of *Lost in the Cosmos. Publishers Weekly* 223 (29 Apr. 1983): 44–45. See also *Publishers Weekly* 225 (20 Apr. 1984): 86.

Romine, Dannye. "Percy Says His Next Work Will Be Nonfiction—and Strange." *Times-Picayune* (N.O.) 23 Jan. 1983: Sect. 3, p. 6.

Ross, Michele. "Percy on One Heck of a Trip." *Atlantic Journal-Constitution* 29 May 1983: 8–H.

Royal, Robert. Rev. of *Lost in the Cosmos. National Review* 35 (16 Sept. 1983): 1149.

Sheppard, R.Z. Rev. of *Lost in the Cosmos. Time* 121 (20 June 1983): 78.

Stokes, Geoffrey. "Dr. Percy's Medicine Show." Rev. of *Lost in the Cosmos. Village Voice* 28 (14 June 1983): 39.

Winchell, Mark Royden. Rev. of *Lost in the Cosmos. American Spectator* 16 (Dec. 1983): 42–43.

"Winners of Times Book Prizes Named." *Los Angeles Times* 19 Nov. 1983: Calendar, Part V, p. 1.

Young, Tracy. Rev. of *Lost in the Cosmos. Rolling Stone* 21 July 1983: 119.

City of the Dead

Kemp, John R. "City of the Dead." *Southeastern* 2 (Summer 1985): 25–27.

Diagnosing the Modern Malaise

Kemp, John R. Rev. of *Diagnosing the Modern Malaise*. *Times-Picayune* (N.O.), 29 Sept. 1985: Sect. C, p. 7.

Novel Writing in an Apocalyptic Time

Simmons, Mabel, "In Praise of A National Asset." *TP/SI* (N.O.), 7 September 1986: Sect. L, p. 6.

The Thanatos Syndrome

Cubbage, Robert. "Writing in the Ruins." *Notre Dame Magazine* (Autumn 1987): 29–31.

Fuller, Edmund. "Death and Modern Morality." *Wall Street Journal* 24 March 1987: 30, 34.

Godwin, Gail. "The Devil's Own Century." *New York Times Book Review* 92 (5 April 1987): 1+.

Gray, Paul. "Implications of Apocalypse." *Time* 129 (30 March 1987): 71.

Jones, Malcolm. "Moralist of the South." *New York Times Magazine* 136 (22 March 1987): 42+.

Reed, Julia. "The Last Southern Gentleman." *U.S. News and World Report* 102 (16 March 1987): 75–76.

Rev. of *The Thanatos Syndrome*. *Library Journal* 112 (15 April 1987): 100+.

Rev. of *The Thanatos Syndrome*. *New Republic* 196 (13 April 1987): 31+.

Rev. of *The Thanatos Syndrome*. *America* 156 (11 April 1987): 308+.

Rev. of *The Thanatos Syndrome*. *Atlantic* 259 (April 1987): 86+.

Rev. of *The Thanatos Syndrome*. *New York Times* 136 (1 April 1987): 19, C-28.

Rev. of *The Thanatos Syndrome*. *Publishers Weekly* 231 (6 Feb. 1987): 86+.

WALKER PERCY, LINDA HOBSON, COVINGTON, LA., 1985

About the Author

Linda Whitney Hobson lives in New Orleans as a writer and teacher. She is at present completing a book on Walker Percy's novels, *Understanding Walker Percy,* to be published by the University of South Carolina Press. She is a book reviewer for the Atlanta *Journal-Constitution* and arts columnist for *Louisiana Life* Magazine. In addition to teaching American literature at Newman School, she does free-lance editing and journalism.